Reading Abbey Records
a new miscellany

for my brother and in memory of my sister

Reading Abbey Records
a new miscellany

Edited by Brian Kemp

Berkshire Record Society
Volume 25
2018

Published by the
Berkshire Record Society
c/o Berkshire Record Office
9 Coley Avenue, Reading
Berkshire
RG1 6AF

in association with
the Friends of Reading Abbey

Printed and bound by
Berforts South West Ltd
17 Burgess Road, Ivyhouse Lane
Hastings, East Sussex, TN35 4NR

ISBN 978-0-9573937-6-9

Contents

	Page
Foreword	v
Acknowledgements	vii
Illustration	viii
Introduction	ix
Abbreviations	xi
THE ANNALS OF READING ABBEY	1
THE MIRACLES OF THE HAND OF ST JAMES	53
HENRY I's ANNIVERSARY	101
SCHEDULE OF FEASTS, ANNIVERSARIES AND PITTANCES	111
Index to persons and places	127
Index to subjects	137

Cover illustration: the Chapter House from the east, part of an engraving published in *Historical Antiquities of England and Wales*, by Henry Boswell and others, 1786

Foreword by the Abbot of Douai

My first view of Reading Abbey came at half-term, February 1963, during one of the worst winters of that time. From a distance, I thought the surviving buildings were magnificent although I couldn't understand why there was so much brick and crenellation. As I walked closer, I realised that I was in fact looking at the Victorian prison, built over much of the abbey, and not at the few blackened, misshapen, and stunted flint remains of the Benedictine abbey, lying in the foreground like a whale's skeleton in the snow. These ruins are all that remains to us of the majestic abbey buildings, and it can be difficult to imagine what they looked like. No illustration is found on seals or in early engravings, although from the records included in this volume we know that there was certainly a tower attached to the abbey church. We know also that it possessed carved stonework of the highest order, much of which, scattered far and wide after the Dissolution, has been painstakingly rescued and collected together, and is now the subject of specialist study. Over the past few decades, the Friends of Reading Abbey-have worked successfully to heighten popular interest in the ruins. The principal achievement of the past century has, however, been twofold: the painstaking archaeological analysis by Cecil Slade, and the awakened interest in the abbey's material culture in terms of its surviving records. Three scholars have been mainly responsible for this latter: Jamieson B. Hurry at the beginning of the twentieth century, Alan Coates at the end of that century, and Professor Brian Kemp, whose longstanding interest in the abbey has straddled both centuries. His major publication was an introduction to, and an edition of, the Reading Abbey Cartularies (1986-87), Over the years, however, he has been quietly examining other documents relating to the abbey, and this volume of the Berkshire Record Society has allowed him to publish here the original Latin texts accompanied by his own translations.

The annals of Reading Abbey found in this volume help to expand our knowledge of this Benedictine community in its heyday. The great French abbey of Cluny inspired Reading to follow its customary and the bond was tightened when Abbot Hugh II of Reading (1186-99) became Abbot Hugh V of Cluny itself (1199-1207), where he achieved fame as a major reformer of that abbey and perhaps made use of talents he had earlier developed at Reading. The annals show how the abbey's original Cluniac affiliation was gradually diluted as English customs were introduced after the Fourth Lateran Council of 1215 encouraged all monasteries to join national congregations. Reading was a royal foundation, the creation of Henry I in 1121, and these annals paint King John his successor in softer colours than he is usually depicted in the popular imagination.

The other documents found in this volume remind us that Reading Abbey was above all else a religious centre, and the daily worship of the monks lay at the heart of its life. It is, therefore, satisfying to have an insight here into its

liturgical feasts and fasts, some of which were shared with its daughter house, the priory at Leominster. From the abbey's liturgical life we glean details of individual benefactors to the abbey, previously unknown, and new facts about the festive meals which accompanied the church liturgy, one being, for instance, the provision of Cholsey ale. The surviving documents brought to our attention in this volume, however, highlight two distinctive features of the monastery's worship and influence. Firstly, the extraordinarily elaborate ceremonial performed each year by the abbot and community to honour King Henry I, the abbey's founder, on the anniversary of his death. And, secondly, the widespread popularity of the cult of the apostle, St. James the Great, thanks to the abbey's prized possession of the relic of his hand. The descriptions of miraculous cures associated with this relic, which we are given here, provide important details of ritual observances which employed water and candles as well as evidence of local religious devotion in Berkshire, notably around Bucklebury.

I welcome this valuable contribution to our understanding of Reading Abbey and hope it will stimulate still further interest in what was the town's most important medieval institution and remains its most important monument.

Abbot Geoffrey Scott
Douai Abbey
15 October 2017

Acknowledgements

The texts in this volume have been published by kind permission of the following: The Provost and Fellows of Worcester College, Oxford (the Annals and the Schedule of Feasts, from Worcester College MS 213); the Librarian of Gloucester Cathedral (the Miracles, from Gloucester Cathedral Library MS 1) and the British Library (the Commemoration of the Anniversary of Henry I, from Add MS 8167). The translation of the Miracles has previously been published in the *Berkshire Archaeological Journal* (volume 65, 1970), and permission to reproduce it here has kindly been given by the Berkshire Archaeological Society.

Berkshire Record Society also gratefully acknowledges a generous contribution towards the costs of publication by the Friends of Reading Abbey, from the Sabina Sutherland bequest.

Reading Abbey: the Chapter House from the Dormitory
(Photograph: David Shephard)

Introduction

This volume comprises four texts which, in different ways, bring Reading Abbey to life. Whereas the abbey's library and its charters have received intensive study, as also its architecture and sculptured stones, the lives and preoccupations of the monks have not shone through these studies and are as a consequence little known. Partly this is because no substantial chronicle from the abbey or any continuous run of financial accounts has come down to us, even though we know, or can plausibly suppose, that both were compiled.

The four texts with which we are concerned are as follows: 1) a third set of Reading annals; 2) an account of the miracles worked by Reading's prized relic, the hand of St James; 3) an account of the ceremonial involved in the monks' annual commemoration of the death of their founder, King Henry I, and, finally, 4) a record of the pittances allowed to the monks to mark the feasts of the Christian year and the anniversaries of a large number of individuals, most of whom were their major benefactors, as well as abbots and certain monastic officials of the abbey. All are printed in their original Latin with an English translation alongside. None has been published before, with the single exception of the Miracles of the hand of St James, of which I published an English translation in the *Berkshire Archaeological Journal* as long ago as 1970. That translation is reprinted here, with permission of the Berkshire Archaeological Society, and with a considerably revised introduction and a small number of corrections to the text and footnotes to take account of more recent scholarship.

Chapter 1 discusses the three surviving sets of historical annals compiled at different dates in the abbey, the earliest two of which have long been in print (one since 1879, the other since 1922), but the third and fullest now appears for the first time. Together these three sets preserve a unique corpus of material, not only about the abbey's history itself, but also relating to a variety of external matters that attracted the notice of the various compilers. The third set, printed here, records a very interesting and important range of factual information, a good deal of which is otherwise unknown. This includes, most importantly, the place where the barons' defiance of King John took place in 1215 as Reading, along with the name of their spokesman on that occasion as Geoffrey the canon, chaplain of Robert Fitz Walter, thus adding a new detail to the story of the lead-up to the granting of Magna Carta. Then there is the notice of Abbot Simon's attendance at the Fourth Lateran Council in Rome that same year, called by Pope Innocent III to launch a massive programme of ecclesiastical reform, the abbot's presence serving to put Reading Abbey right at the heart of the universal church. These annals also record the lightning strike on the abbey in 1209 and the severe damage it caused to the fabric, which was also mentioned in the second set of annals but in much less detail.

Chapter 2, on the miracles of St James's hand, contains material that is

already well known from my earlier translation published last century, but whose original Latin text is now printed for the first time. It gives the reader an insight into the extraordinary range of illnesses and inflictions that were cured by the hand's power, too many to cite here, which throw light incidentally on various aspects of contemporary life, including the milking of sheep and the belief in the efficacy of precious stones to ease childbirth. The last two chapters, though shorter than the first two, are no less valuable.

Chapter 3, concerned with the abbey's yearly celebration of Henry I's anniversary, contains important confirmatory evidence for the location of the king's tomb – within the choir of the abbey church, to the west of the High Altar - and a fairly detailed account of the ceremonial and liturgy employed on the eve of the anniversary of his death and on the day itself and, less fully, on the first two days of each month throughout the year. Though not full orders of proceeding, these accounts are perhaps full enough to allow enactments to be performed. The text in chapter 4, unique among the abbey's surviving records, contains lists of the pittances allowed to the monks throughout the year; these are arranged, firstly, by the feasts of the Christian year and, secondly, by the anniversaries of the abbey's chief benefactors, giving altogether a remarkably complete idea of this aspect of life in the abbey in the late thirteenth century.

Grateful thanks are due to the friends and fellow scholars from whose help I have benefited greatly in the preparation of this volume, including Professor David Crouch, Professor Anne Curry, Dom Geoffrey Scott, abbot of Douai, Mark Bainbridge, Librarian of Worcester College, Oxford, and the late Denis Bethell, who many years ago first introduced me to the miracles of St James's hand. Finally, I owe a particular debt of gratitude to Dr Peter Durrant, general editor of the Berkshire Record Society, who has been so helpful in the final stages of the project and has, with great kindness, seen the volume so efficiently through the press. All remaining errors and infelicities remain mine alone.

Brian Kemp
January 2018

Abbreviations used in the notes

Annales Monastici	*Annales Monastici*, ed. H. R. Luard, 5 vols, Rolls Series, London, 1864-9.
'Annales Radingenses'	'Annales Radingenses', ed. F. Liebermann, in *Ungedruckte anglo-normannische Geschichtsquellen*, Strassburg 1879, reprinted 1966.
'Annales Radingenses Posteriores'	'Annales Radingenses Posteriores, 1135-1264', ed. C. W. Previté-Orton, *English Historical Review* 37 (1922), 400-403.
Becket Materials	*Materials for the History of Archbishop Thomas Becket .....*, ed. J. C. Robertson and J. B. Sheppard, 7 vols, Rolls Series, London, 1875-85.
Coates, *English Medieval Books*	A. Coates, *English Medieval Books. The Reading Abbey Collections from Foundation to Dispersal,* Oxford 1999.
Councils and Synods, II (i)	*Councils and Synods, with other documents relating to the English Church*, vol. II, part i, *1205-1265*, ed. F. M. Powicke and C.R. Cheney, Oxford 1964.
EEA	*English Episcopal Acta*, published by the British Academy; vols cited: IX *Winchester 1205*-1238, ed. N. Vincent (1994); 18 *Salisbury 1087-1217*, ed. B. R. Kemp (1999); 35 *Hereford 1234-1275*, ed. J. Barrow (2009); 36 *Salisbury 1229-1262*, ed. B. R. Kemp (2010).
Mayer, *Crusades*	H. E. Mayer, trans. J. Gillingham, *The Crusades*, 2nd edition, Oxford 1988.
Matthew Paris, *Chronica Majora*	*Matthaei Parisiensis, Monachi Sancti Albani, Chronica Majora*, ed. H. R. Luard, 7 vols, Rolls Series, London 1872-83.
Norgate	K. Norgate, *John Lackland*, London 1902.
Painter	S. Painter, *The Reign of King John*, Baltimore 1949.
PL	*Patrologiae cursus completus, series Latina,* ed. J. P. Migne, 221 vols, Paris 1844-64.

Poole	A. L. Poole, *From Domesday Book to Magna Carta*, 2nd edition, Oxford 1955.
Powicke	F. M. Powicke, *The Thirteenth Century 1216-1307*, Oxford 1953.
Reading Cartularies	*Reading Abbey Cartularies*, ed. B. R. Kemp, 2 vols, Camden 4th Series, 31, 33 (1986-7).
Warren	W. L. Warren, *King John*, London 1961.

The annals of Reading Abbey

One sometimes hears it said that the monks of Reading Abbey were not particularly interested in history – and it is certainly true that the abbey produced no great monastic chronicler like William of Malmesbury of Malmesbury Abbey or Jocelin of Brakelond of Bury St Edmunds Abbey, much less a school of historians such as we find at St Albans, with Roger of Wendover and Matthew Paris in the 13th century and Thomas Walsingham in the 14th and 15th centuries. Nevertheless, that is not the whole story, for there is plenty of evidence to show that, especially in the 12th and 13th centuries, some of the Reading monks were sufficiently interested in historical events or historical matters, whether of the nation at large or simply of their own abbey and neighbourhood, to want to write down a record of them. Moreover, we know from the late 12th-century library list, preserved in the abbey's earliest surviving cartulary, the so-called Fingall Cartulary (now British Library, Egerton MS 3031), that the monks possessed a 'History of Reading' which, with 'the deeds of Henry I', was contained in a single volume; it is beyond doubt, I think, that both the History and the account of Henry I, the abbey's founder, were written by a monk or monks of the abbey in the course of the 12th century.[1] Most regrettably, this volume has not come down to us, and we know virtually nothing of its contents, although it is possible that it was seen, or perhaps borrowed, by Matthew Paris of St Albans and that this circumstance explains the unique references he makes to events involving Reading's Hand of St James in the 12th century, references which are likely to have originated with Reading Abbey itself and which, I believe, he took from this lost 'History of Reading'. Thus, it is Matthew Paris alone who informs us that in 1136 Henry, bishop of Winchester, brother of the new king, Stephen, removed St James's Hand from Reading and that it was not restored until the beginning of Henry II's reign in 1155.[2] The Hand of St James is undoubtedly the most famous of the abbey's relics, and we know that it was first sent to Reading by Henry I, who died in 1135, but the cult of the Hand did not begin really to develop until the reign of Henry II (1154-1189), which is at first puzzling;[3] however, this removal of the hand from Reading for the previous twenty years provides the explanation.

The monks of Reading, like other religious, were not averse to jotting down notes of various kinds, including historical notes, in the margins or flyleaves of their manuscript books. Occasionally thereby, they preserve historical information which is not otherwise known. A case in point is the 13th-century Reading Abbey manuscript, now in Lambeth Palace Library,

1. Coates, *English Medieval Books,* 28, 42.
2. MatthewParis, *Chronica Majora,* ii. 164, 210.
3. Brian Kemp, 'The Hand of St James at Reading Abbey', *Saints and Saints' Lives; Essays in Honour of D. H. Farmer* (Reading Medieval Studies XVI, Reading, 1990), 77-96, at 84-5.

London, ms 371; this is a miscellaneous volume mostly of well-known chronicles, but also of other sorts of text, not in itself particularly remarkable but for some extraordinarily interesting notes that it contains.[4] One of these provides unique evidence as to the burial place within the abbey church of King Henry I and his second wife (and widow), Queen Adeliza.[5] In the nature of a memorandum, it reads (in translation):

> William earl of Lincoln married Queen Adeliza, wife of our founder, as is evident in a charter and confirmation of the same William. Accordingly the king's council would not permit her to lie with him [meaning Henry I] in the middle of the presbytery before the altar. She lies buried, however, on the north side of the choir between two columns, apart from King Henry I, our founder and her husband, on whose souls may God have mercy. Amen.

Between these two poles of historical writing, as it were, chronicles and historical jottings, come annals – historical annals – comprising sets of usually brief historical records arranged in a chronological sequence, but without any particular overall theme and often combining events of a national and of a purely local significance. Reading Abbey has left us three sets of such annals, relating respectively to the 11th and 12th centuries, the 12th and 13th centuries, and the 13th century. The first two of these sets have been published, the third not until now.

The earliest surviving annals of Reading Abbey are contained in a volume now in the British Library, Royal ms 8E. XVIII, at folios 94v-96v. They were published in Germany in 1879 by F. Liebermann, who called them 'Annales Radingenses' and included them in a collection of hitherto unpublished English historical sources under the title *Ungedrukte anglo-normannische Geschichtsquellen.*[6] Covering the period 1066-1189, and written in three different hands, these annals were entered in the margin of an Easter Table, and most of them are in consequence very short. Despite their very lean and jejune nature, however, they preserve priceless information which we simply should not have otherwise. It is these annals which tell us, for example, when the first monks arrived and where they had come from. The famous annal, under the year 1121, is worth quoting in translation in full:[7]

> Peter, the prior, and seven brethren with him were sent to England by Abbot Pons of Cluny at the request of King Henry and, joined by several brethren from the monastery of St Pancras, began the observance of the Cluniac order in the monastery newly founded by the king, on the 14th kalend of July [i. e., 18 June].

Two years later, under the year 1123, we read that 'Hugh, formerly prior of

4. Coates, *English Medieval Books,* 156, no. 65.
5. M. R. James, *Catalogue of the Mediaeval Manuscripts in the Library of Lambeth Palace* (Cambridge, 1932), 503.
6. 'Annales Radingenses', 9-12. A facsimile of one folio of the manuscript is reproduced in J. and C. Hillaby, *Leominster Minster, Priory and Borough c. 660-1539* (Leominster, 2006), 138.
7. 'Annales Radingenses', 11.

Lewes, was appointed first abbot of Reading (and) prior Peter returned to Cluny'.[8] These two laconic annals really speak paragraphs about the changing ideas and negotiations surrounding the earliest monastic establishment at Reading. We are able to detect a distinct change of plan after the first monks arrived, for it looks very much as though Reading was thought of initially by the abbot of Cluny, if not by the king, as a priory under the authority of the abbot of Cluny, but that, under pressure mainly from the king, it was decided to raise the new house to abbatial status and to appoint an abbot, with the consequence, as the king certainly intended, that Reading from 1123 was now an independent Cluniac abbey and not a Cluniac priory subordinate to the abbot of Cluny.[9]

We are also largely dependent on these annals for the succession of the first three abbots of Reading: Hugh just mentioned (1123-1130), Anscher (1130-1135) and Edward (1136-*c.*1154). The exact date of Henry I's burial in the abbey in 1136 is correctly given as the nones of January [i.e. 5 January], which is in conflict with the oft-stated date of 4 January,[10] but is corroborated by two other reliable sources.[11] Moreover, under the year 1139 we have a crucial annal describing the commencement of full monastic life in the abbey's dependent priory at Leominster (Herefordshire): 'In the same year', we read in translation, 'prior Joseph, sent to Leominster by abbot Edward, vigorously inaugurated the observance of the order there.'[12] We know from the abbey's cartularies that Henry I had given the Reading monks the old defunct nunnery of Leominster and its lands by 1123 at the latest,[13] but it is this annal alone that enables us to date the foundation of the fully conventual priory there in 1139.

On the other hand, since they are annals and the monks who wrote them were inevitably selective in what they chose to record, much other information which we should like to have is not there. We look in vain in these annals, for example, for any notice of the arrival of the Hand of St James in Reading. The 'Annales Radingenses' record the Empress Matilda's return to England from Germany in 1126, but, although one might have expected the annal to add that she brought back the Hand of St James with her, it is silent on the matter.

The second set of Reading annals was entered in a volume which is now in the Library of St John's College, Cambridge, ms A. 22, written in the 13th century and mostly devoted to a copy of the Venerable Bede's *De*

8. *Ibid.*
9. See *Reading Cartularies*, i. 14-15.
10. 'Annales Radingenses', 11. For the earlier dating, see *Reading Cartularies*, i. 14, note 1.
11. 'Winchcombe Annals 1094-1181', ed. R. R. Darlington, in *A Medieval Miscellany for Doris Mary Stenton*, ed. P. M. Barnes and C. F. Slade , (Pipe Roll Society, new series xxxvi, 1962), 127; *The Chronicle of John of Worcester*, ed. and trans., P. McGurk, iii (Oxford Medieval Texts, Oxford, 1998), 214, year 1136, textual note *c.*
12. 'Annales Radingenses', 11.
13. *Reading Cartularies*, i. 16 and no.1.

temporibus. Like the first set of Reading annals, these, too, were entered in the margin of an Easter Table. They were published under the name 'Annales Radingenses Posteriores' by C. W. Previté-Orton in *The English Historical Review*, volume 37 (1922).[14] Beginning in 1135 with the death of Henry I, although the sequence does not start in earnest until 1148, they end in 1264 with the Battle of Lewes between Henry III and Simon de Montfort and his supporters, but the last entry concerning the battle has been largely erased. A succession of five different monks had a hand in writing the annals, and the composition of each annal seems to have been roughly contemporary with the events described. The early sections overlap with the first set of annals, but there appears to be no connection between the two sets. The comment made above regarding the earlier set and the Hand of St James applies equally to the second set of annals, for from the latter, too, we get no inkling that the Hand was ever in Reading, despite the fact that the cult of the relic reached its apogee in the period covered by them. Nevertheless, the material they do present is of immense interest and importance locally, even though hardly anything significant in national affairs is reported that we do not otherwise know of, justifying in this respect the editor's rather dismissive remark that 'they have not much of interest'. For local matters, on the other hand, there is 'much of interest'. In the first place, these annals are fundamental in establishing the succession and dates of the abbots of Reading, especially in the second half of the twelfth century, even if some of the information occurs also in the 13th-century *Flores Historiarum* of Matthew Paris,[15] who, as we saw, probably had access to the abbey's 'History of Reading'. What is utterly unique to these annals, however, is the notice that abbot Joseph, who became abbot in 1173, did not die or otherwise give up the abbacy in 1180, as suggested by J. B. Hurry, the abbey's celebrated historian, but resigned in 1186 and eventually died on 8th February 1191.[16] We need to remember that, when Hurry's history was published in 1901, these annals had not yet found their way into print. For the first half of the 13th century, although the succession of abbots is generally known from other sources, it is mainly to these annals that we owe the exact dates of death or the equivalent; even so, the entries are otherwise very uninformative - a typical example is the annal for 1261 (or 1262 by modern dating): 'Master Richard of Chichester, abbot of Reading, died on the 11th kalend of April (i.e., 22 March); Richard Bannister succeeded him.'[17]

Most importantly, however, these annals are the only source for the exact date of the dedication of the abbey church by Archbishop Thomas Becket on 19 April, 1164. The relevant annal reads: 'Dedication of the church of Reading by St Thomas, archbishop of Canterbury and martyr, on the 13th

14. 'Annales Radingenses Posteriores', 400-3.
15. *Flores Historiarum*, ed. H. R. Luard, (3 vols, Rolls Series, London, 1890).
16. 'Annales Radingenses Posteriores', 401; J. B. Hurry, *Reading Abbey*, (London, 1901), 30, 111; British Library, Cotton MS Vespasian E v (Reading Almoner's cartulary), fo. 12r.
17. 'Annales Radingenses Posteriores', 403.

kalend of May (i.e. 19 April)'.[18] Other records from outside Reading are confused or imprecise on the date - the annals of both Bermondsey and Winchester give the year only, as 1164 (Bermondsey) or 1163 (Winchester). Matthew Paris also has the correct year, 1164,[19] but the extraneous chronicler who comes closest to the dating in the Reading annals is the contemporary and well-informed Norman writer, Robert of Torigny, who gives the date as 1164 'around the octave of Easter';[20] now, the octave of Easter in 1164 was 19 April, as recorded in our annals. That this precise date is correct we can be certain, since it was customary to dedicate monastic and cathedral churches on Sundays. It is interesting to note, however, that our entry cannot have been written strictly at the time of the event, for it refers to the archbishop as 'St Thomas and martyr', whereas he was not martyred until 29 December 1170 and not canonised until February 1173.[21]

Violent or unusual weather occurrences are reported in these annals, as is commonly true of other annals and chronicles, the most important in the present case being the record of a flash of lightning which hit the abbey church on 12 March 1209 and set fire to it.[22] As we shall see, this devastating and destructive 'act of God' was also recorded in Reading's third surviving set of annals, which supply more details of the damage.[23] These annals also contain useful indications of Reading Abbey's relationship with Prince John, Richard I's younger brother, a relationship that was to blossom into a deeper and mutually beneficial association and regard after he became king in 1199. In 1191, we are told, Prince John gave the abbey a gold cup worth 5 marks, or £3 6s 8d in old currency, and in 1192 the annals record John's gift of one mark of gold annually, a very handsome gift, which we know from charter evidence was designed to compensate the monks for the loss of the gold reliquary of the Hand of St James, which his brother, King Richard, had taken from Reading in 1189 when about to leave on Crusade.[24] Most of this detail is not given in the annals, but it is the annals alone which supply the date.

The annals also record the dedication of the new cathedral of Salisbury, which was the cathedral of the diocese to which Berkshire belonged in the Middle Ages, as taking place in 1258 on the feast of St Michael (29 September).[25] The annals thus join two other 13th-century monastic sources within the diocese, and two outside it, in giving the date as 29 September, whereas the anniversary of the dedication was celebrated annually on 30

18. *Ibid,* 400.
19. *Annales Monastici*, iii. 441-2; ii. 57; Matthew Paris, *Chronica Majora,* ii. 227.
20. 'The Chronicle of Robert of Torigny', in *Chronicles of the Reigns of Stephen, Henry II and Richard I*, ed. R. Howlett, (4 vols, Rolls Series, London, 1884-9), iv. 221.
21. F. Barlow, *Thomas Becket*, (London, 1986), 1, 247, 269.
22. 'Annales Radingenses Posteriores', 401.
23. See below, p. 12.
24. 'Annales Radingenses Posteriores', 401; *Reading Cartularies*, i. nos. 42, 46.
25. 'Annales Radingenses Posteriores', 403.

September,[26] leading many people in later years to believe that the dedication itself had been on 30 September.

We come now to the third set of surviving Reading Abbey annals, which has hitherto existed only in manuscript form and is published here for the first time. These annals seem not to have been at all widely known or studied, certainly not for what they have to tell us about the history of the abbey. They are to be found in a 13th-century manuscript in the Library of Worcester College, Oxford.[27] It is a fascinating manuscript which contains, in addition to the annals, liturgical and devotional material, copies of certain works by St Jerome and St Anselm and, most interestingly and apparently not found elsewhere, graded lists of the feasts of the Church's year in order of status from the abbey's point of view, and the allowances of wine and ale and special dishes permitted to the Reading monks on these occasions.[28] For example, the first list of nine feasts, called 'the principal double feasts', comprises the Annunciation, the Dedication of the abbey church, Easter, Whitsun, SS Peter and Paul, St James the Great, the Assumption of St Mary, Christmas and St John the Evangelist, for which the monks were allowed extra measures of wine and seven dishes, including flans; for another group of feasts they were permitted six dishes, including lozenges or flans and rissoles.[29] There is also a list of the ten days when the sub-prior was obliged to provide a meal for the convent, evidently to mark the anniversaries of distinguished persons who died on those days, including here Giles (of Bridport), bishop of Salisbury,[30] and a much longer list of the days when the chamberlain had to do the same for the commemoration of others, including most notably King Henry the founder, for whom he was to do it on the eve of the king's anniversary and on the day itself.[31]

At the top of page 2 of this manuscript there is a note stating that it was given to the abbey by Alan, the prior, who, we know, was certainly in office in 1290 and is perhaps to be identified with the prior A. who occurs in December 1279. It is thought that prior Alan may have compiled the annals in their present form and perhaps also the list of feasts.[32] Unlike the first two sets of annals, these annals are not written in the margin of an Easter Table, but stand independent on the page, a circumstance which allows them in general to be longer and more expansive than the earlier sets. They run in the same hand from 1199, the death of Richard I, to 1281, but curiously not in a continuous series. They certainly run continuously from 1199 to 1264 (on pages 10-22), but then there is a break in the chronology and the annals resume with the year 1276, even more strangely, written on two earlier pages,

26. See *EEA,* 36, *Salisbury 1229-1262*, xliii-xliv.
27. Worcester College, Oxford, MS 213.
28. *Ibid,* 7-9.
29. These lists are both *ibid*, 7.
30. *Ibid,* 8.
31. *Ibid*, 9.
32. Coates, *English Medieval Books,* 71; *Reading Cartularies*, i. no. 230.

3 and 4, with an additional annal for 1277 incongruously inserted over an erasure on page 2. In fact, it is perfectly clear that we are not dealing here with a fair copy, but the result of a project that seems to have been left unfinished and, moreover, suffered, from a change of plan in the course of its composition. It appears that the original idea was to have a set of annals beginning on page 1 with the year 1000, but, after marking out the first two pages with the required dates, only a few entries were made on these pages and those on page 2 were subsequently erased to allow other writing to take place. Moreover, a distinct change in the character of the annals is observable from 1242 onwards, for they are now much shorter and far more sketchy than the preceding annals. For example, the annal for 1246 simply says:

> Robert, bishop of Salisbury, died and W(illiam) of York succeeded him. Item Walter Marshal died.[33]

No annals at all are recorded for the years 1248, 1251, 1256 and 1259 and, to repeat, there is a complete break between 1264 and 1277. It is true that some annals after 1242 are a little more substantial, but even these prove on analysis to be little more than a series of bald facts without usually much elaboration or discussion, interesting though many of the facts are in themselves. My tentative conclusion about these annals is, therefore, that prior Alan, or whoever it was who compiled the set as we have it, made use of a set of fairly full annals running down to 1241 and of some sketchy notes for the subsequent period down to 1264, and made what looks like a rather half-hearted attempt to resume the annals in 1276, which in turn fizzled out in 1281.

However, it is important not to minimise the interest of these annals, for they preserve a great deal of information on some important aspects of the abbey's history in the 13th century. The author of the first and most significant part of the annals had a fairly eclectic approach to what he recorded, although he seems to have been particularly interested in the English royal family, including its relations with the rulers of Scotland and Wales, some foreign ruling houses, Crusading events in the Mediterranean or the Holy Land when he heard of them, notably, for instance, the surrender of Jerusalem to the Emperor Frederick II by the Moslems in 1229;[34] closer to home, his interest was engaged by events involving the abbey or its abbots, the weather and the heavenly bodies (a perennial preoccupation of medieval annalists and chroniclers, of course), but he largely avoids serious political polemic. The later, more sketchy, annalist seems to have been especially concerned to record deaths of monks of Reading, a number of whom were evidently obedientiaries (almoner, infirmarian, and so on), although he does not say so.

It is well known that, since Reading Abbey had been founded by a king, Henry I, it was and remained a royal abbey. This meant that every subsequent

33. Below, p. 42.
34. Below, p. 33.

king of England was patron of the abbey, and this in turn, coupled with its wealth and size and the geographical position of Reading, meant that kings and royalty often came to, and stayed in, the abbey. That being said, however, the monks certainly had closer links with some kings than with others, and none more so than with King John – bad King John, as the monks of St Albans and others would have said and as the popular image of the king remains to this day, but I am sure that the monks of Reading (or at least many of them) would not have agreed. We have already seen the evidence in the second set of Reading annals for Prince John's generosity to the monks, and much more could be added from other sources. Now I want to focus on two of the annals in this third set of Reading annals which bring the relationship between John and the abbey into sharp relief. It has always been known from many other sources that King John had a high regard for the abbey's most prized relic, the Hand of St James, but quite how much he valued it in practical terms is brought out very clearly in the annal for 1200.[35] This states that, among the religious relics on which Philip II of France swore to maintain peace with John when they met at Les Andelys on the Norman border in France, was the Hand of St James. John had evidently arranged for the Hand to be taken to Normandy for the ceremony – the first time, incidentally, that we know of the relic leaving England since it was brought from Germany by the Empress Matilda in 1126 – because he valued its spiritual power and wished to harness it to strengthen the force of Philip's oath. Moreover, we know from elsewhere that the ceremony took place on Ascension Day (18 May in 1200), the first anniversary of John's coronation and a feast of the highest significance for him.[36] The peace and oath-swearing at Andelys formed the prelude to the Treaty of Le Goulet on 22 May, which embodied their terms. However, if John had hoped thus to use the Hand to guarantee Philip II's good faith, he was disappointed, for, as the annal goes on to say, Philip began to attack Normandy within two years and had overrun the Duchy by the summer of 1204.[37] Nonetheless, the episode enables us to add another paragraph to our knowledge of the Hand of St James.

The second annal connecting John and the abbey is that for the fateful year of 1215, in which the king was eventually constrained to grant Magna Carta. The annal fills out very significantly what we know about the formal opening of hostilities between the rebel barons and the king. It states that:

> The barons of England defied King John at Reading by Geoffrey, canon and chaplain of Robert Fitz Walter, summoning and gathering his accomplices and conspirators at Northampton around the feast of St James [the Less, 1 May] at Northampton.[38]

This annal thus definitively locates the barons' *diffidatio,* or renunciation of

35. Below, p. 17.
36. Norgate, 73.
37. Warren, 93-9.
38. Below, p. 25.

homage, at Reading, and this is confirmed by the annals of Southwark and another source, but the Dunstable annals, usually well-informed, give the place as Wallingford.[39] More importantly, the annal supplies the name of the representative who spoke on behalf of the barons, hitherto unknown, as 'Geoffrey the canon'. The Southwark annals tell us that it was a black canon (at this time probably an Augustinian canon), but Reading alone supplies his name; since he is described also as a chaplain to Robert Fitz Walter, one of whose principal estates was at Dunmow (Essex), Geoffrey may well have been a canon of the Augustinian priory of Little Dunmow, of which Robert Fitz Walter was patron.[40] The Reading annal gives no precise date for the *diffidatio*, but implies perhaps that it followed soon after the feast of St James the Less (1 May); the Southwark annals date the renunciation of homage to the vigil of St John at the Latin Gate, i.e., 5 May, and John is known to have been in Reading from 2 to 6 May, moving to London by 7 May.[41] There is thus no reason to question the accuracy and reliability of the details supplied in the Reading annal.

Some years later the abbey was indirectly affected by the conflict between John's successor, King Henry III, and his rebellious barons in the middle of the thirteenth century. A succinct annal of 1263 reports an event in Reading, which is not otherwise known but which cannot easily be dismissed on that account, given its local reference. It states baldly that around 24 June the barons began to attack the enemies of the kingdom (namely, the king's favourites), and on 29 June came in arms to Reading.[42] No further details are given, but in the following year, 1264, the annals record the famous Battle of Lewes between the king and the barons which took place on 14 May and resulted in total victory for the barons.[43] As noted above, the second set of Reading annals had originally ended with an account of the battle, which was subsequently largely erased.[44] It is also very relevant that the only surviving text of the so-called 'Song of Lewes', which celebrates the defeat of the Crown by the barons in this battle, is contained in the same Reading Abbey manuscript which contains the music and text of the 'Reading Round', *Sumer is icumen in*.[45] It looks very much as though, despite its royal foundation,

39. M. Tyson, 'The Annals of Southwark and Merton', *Surrey Archaeological Collections*, xxxi (1925), 49; *De Antiquis Legibus Liber*, ed. T. Stapleton, (Camden Society, London, 1846), 201; for the Dunstable Annals, see *Annales Monastici*, iii. 43 (wrongly dated to 1214).

40. *Victoria History of the County of Essex*, (1907), ii. 151.

41. *Rotuli Litterarum Patentium* ... (1201-1216), vol. I (i), ed. T. D. Hardy, (Record Commission, 1835), 134-5.

42. Below, p. 47. The Dunstable Annals record the king calling a parliament at Reading in 1263, but this is not otherwise known and the reference may perhaps be due to confusion over the nature of the baronial gathering in Reading. For the movements of the barons in 1263, see *Documents of the Baronial Movement of Reform and Rebellion 1258-1267*, ed. R. F. Treharne and I. J. Sanders, (Oxford, 1973), 42.

43. Below, p. 47

44. See above, p. 4.

45. Coates, *English Medieval Books*, 162, no. 97; see also *ibid,* 72, 75.

there was a group or faction among the Reading monks at this time which was critical of Henry III and supportive of the reforming agenda of Simon de Montfort and his baronial supporters. The baronial visit in arms to Reading in June 1263 may, therefore, point to this disaffection at Reading almost a year before the battle. Be that as it may, however, the subsequent royal victory at Evesham in 1265 saw the royalist stance of the abbey fully restored and the erasure noted above.

There are also in these annals some illuminating comments on certain of the abbots. The annal for 1199 reports the elevation of abbot Hugh II to the abbacy of Cluny itself, with the following glowing tribute to his time at Reading: 'He ruled the monastic order with vigour for fourteen years, in many ways he enlarged the buildings and expanded the worship and revenues, and in several ways greatly improved the state of the monastery.' His successor, abbot Elias, is given an even more generous encomium: 'A man praiseworthy in all things, a particular lover of the house of God, who acquired magnificent ornaments for the house of God, and an assiduous preserver of the peace of the convent and the order.'[46] There may be an element of exaggeration in these testimonials, of course, but, on the other hand, abbot Hugh II must have possessed extraordinary qualities to have been elected abbot of Cluny, one of the greatest and most famous abbeys in Christendom, and the nuns of Wintney priory (Hants) regarded abbot Elias as one of their benefactors.[47] Moreover, the annal for 1204 reports that Elias allowed Laurence Burgeys, bailiff of the town of Reading, to build a chapel in honour of Edmund the Martyr, adjacent to which he made himself a hermit, this being the origin of St Edmund's chapel, which stood at the western end of what is now Friar Street, near to where the Franciscan friary was to be built in 1285, and which fell out of use in the 15th century.[48] The fullest and most important information, however, is recorded for Elias's successor, Simon, who became abbot in 1213. It was a further mark of King John's favour to the abbey that, as the Dunstable annals relate, a successor to abbot Elias was appointed immediately on his death without the intervention of royal custody;[49] our annals bear this out, stating that Elias died on 21 July and Simon was appointed on 31 July, a mere ten days later, an exceptionally short interval at any time, but especially so at this time when the papal interdict in England was in force and most vacant abbeys were retained in royal custody. It shows, arguably, that John did not want one of his favourite and most trusted monastic communities to be without a head for longer than absolutely necessary. In fact, abbot Simon was to be employed on a number of diplomatic and other missions by John and his successor, Henry III. The first evidence of his acting as a royal agent occurs in the annal for 1214,[50] where

46. Below, p. 17.
47. British Library, Cotton MS Claudius D. iii, fo. 153v.
48. Below, p. 19.
49. *Annales Monastici,* iii. 38-9.
50. Below, p. 25.

we learn of the potential dangers inherent in such service. Part of the annal tells how Simon went to France to the imprisoned earl of Salisbury; on his return his ship was lost at Wissant along with a large part of his gear, and six of his household servants were drowned, the rest just managing to survive. This annal contains very important information not preserved elsewhere. The earl of Salisbury was the great William Longespée, illegitimate half-brother of the king and for most of his career a staunch supporter of him. He commanded an English expedition to Flanders in 1214, on behalf of King John and in alliance with the king of Germany against Philip II of France, and led the English forces at the fateful Battle of Bouvines, fought on 27 July 1214.[51] The result was a resounding victory for Philip II and, although he was not present, a disastrous defeat for John. More immediately, the earl of Salisbury was captured and imprisoned by the French, and, although we have no details, it looks very much as though abbot Simon was despatched as an envoy to him in prison, a mission which we know of thanks only to these annals. Equally unique to them is the notice under the year 1215 that abbot Simon attended the Fourth Lateran Council called by Pope Innocent III in Rome and was there from 1 November 1215 to 22 February 1216.[52] This was undoubtedly the greatest of the series of Lateran Councils for the whole Church which popes had held in Rome since 1123, and it launched a massive programme of church reform, whose working-out took much of the rest of the thirteenth century.[53] Our annalist says that 900 abbots attended, a figure larger than other estimates of around 800, but one he may have obtained from abbot Simon himself on his return; at any rate, it is gratifying to know that the abbot of Reading was present and able to meet churchmen and religious from all parts of Europe.

As mentioned earlier, these annals reveal a certain interest of the compiler in the weather and the heavenly bodies. For example, the annal of 1222 reports that a comet appeared in the western sky with an amazingly long tail stretching out to the south, and this was followed by a great wind which uprooted many trees and overturned towers and houses; unfortunately, he does not supply a more exact date.[54] In 1230 an eclipse of the moon on 21st November is recorded, and in 1232 a hugely swollen river on 20th March, when the Kennet and Loddon overflowed their banks and many people feared that the Flood was come.[55] Another deluge occurred in 1240, when, according to our annalist, half the bridge between Reading and Caversham (the only Thames crossing in the neighbourhood at this time) collapsed and was almost destroyed as a result of the serious and frequent flooding.[56] The most terrible

51. Warren, 223-4.
52. Below, pp. 25-27.
53. See M. Gibbs and J. Lang, *Bishops and Reform 1215- 1272, (*Oxford, 1934).
54. Below, p. 31. The annals of Waverley and of Dunstable both record this comet and date it to the autumn (Waverley) or the winter (Dunstable) *Annales Monastici*, ii. 297; iii. 77.
55. Below, p. 35.
56. Below, p. 39.

natural occurrence reported in the annals, however, is the one that I mentioned earlier from the 'Annales Radingenses Posteriores', namely, the flash of lightning which struck the abbey church in 1209. The version here is considerably fuller than the earlier notice.[57] Now we read that on the feast of St Gregory (12 March) a dark whirlwind engulfed the entire church of Reading, and then a flash of lightning suddenly descended and flew around the tower of the church before striking and setting fire, first, to the north side of the church and then to the south side. This was clearly a terrifying event, and the shock and horror it kindled in the hearts of the monks is vividly portrayed in the annal, but quite how much actual destruction it wrought on the abbey's fabric is not clear – for example, no part of the church is said to have collapsed. The annal's unqualified reference to the church's tower, which probably means the central, crossing tower, suggests that that was the only tower or, if not, that it was so prominent (over, say, any western towers) as to befit its being described as 'the tower of the church'.

None of the other abbots in the period covered by these annals receives any sort of extended treatment, beyond the bare record of their appointment and death. On the diocesan front Bishop Richard Poore's removal of the see of Salisbury from Old Sarum to New Salisbury is recorded correctly under 1220, the year in which, as is known from a Salisbury source, the foundation stones of the new cathedral were laid,[58] but the annal gives the date incorrectly as 14 February, the correct date being 28 April, as stated in the Salisbury source. In any case, our annal must have assumed its present form some years after 1220, since it adds that 'now the fabric of the church has been nobly built'. The affairs of the abbey's dependent priory of Leominster in Herefordshire figure from time to time in the annals, mainly in references to the priory or to the bishops of Hereford. The most extensive is the annal for 1207, which reveals the outrage felt at Reading at an action by the bishop of Hereford.[59] It tells how he entered the chapter house at Leominster in an attempt to change the status of the priory and to make it subject to his authority, that he was ignominiously repulsed and eventually managed to make an honourable peace and that his action had so offended St Peter, patron of Leominster, that his supporters were condemned to either prison or exile and were deprived of their wealth. The vehemence of the annalist's outrage is striking. This episode does not appear to have been reported elsewhere, but is readily comprehensible in a Reading context, for it helps to explain why, after the bishop had died and the upheavals of John's reign were over, the next bishop of Hereford, in 1217 or 1218, confirmed the abbot of Reading's complete control over monastic affairs at Leominster and the appointment of its priors, since there is otherwise no obvious reason why the

57. Below, p. 21. It appears in the manuscript for 1208. See p. 15, below, for a note on dating.
58. Below, p. 29; *Vetus registrum Sarisberiense alias dictum registrum S Osmundi episcopei*, ed. W. H. R. Jones, (2 vols, Rolls Series, London, 1883-4), ii. 12.
59. Below, pp. 19-21.

bishop should have issued the confirmation at this time.[60] The annal provides the missing link, for it shows that, in order to avoid any repetition of the events of 1207, Reading Abbey realised the need to secure written episcopal confirmation of the rights it had long claimed to exercise at Leominster. We know, too, that it had the grant confirmed by the pope and by later bishops of Hereford.[61]

A most extraordinary annal occurs under the year 1255.[62] It relates that on 28th September, Hubert, dean of Leominster, came to Reading and gave considerable sums of money to the chamber and the infirmary, with smaller sums to individual monks, as well as paying off the kitchen's debt of over £9, all in addition to the £818 given over the previous ten years. In understanding this annal, one needs to realise that the title 'dean' was an alternative title to that of prior, which the head of Leominster Priory habitually bore to emphasise the priory's dependency on Reading Abbey, the very thing that had been challenged by the bishop of Hereford in 1207.[63] Hubert occurs in at least one charter in the Leominster cartulary in the mid-13th century,[64] but nothing else dates him so precisely as this annal. The reference to his coming to Reading in 1255 may perhaps point to his retirement from office, to live out his remaining days in the parent house, and, if the ten years over which he had given the £818 refers to his time as dean, or prior, of Leominster, he would have assumed that office in 1245. Little of this is certain, however, and there remains the problem of the huge sums he had conveyed to the abbey, amounting to some £1161, unless perhaps they conceal arrears in the annual pension, or payment, due from Leominster Priory to Reading abbey, which by 1291 was set at £240.[65]

One more annal, out of the many others in this third set of Reading annals, deserves to be highlighted. Among the rather disordered annals which bring the series to a close is a later addition to the short annal for 1277 on page 3 of the manuscript, which, as stated above, is written over an earlier erasure on page 2. Although it is in some respects confused, it enables us to date and locate a meeting of Benedictine abbots held in Reading Abbey between 15 and 17 September, 1277, and looks forward to a new period in the history of the order in England.[66] The annal tells us, moreover, that forty-five abbots were present – one can only imagine the catering, lodging and stabling arrangements that such a gathering would have necessitated. As is well

60. *Reading Cartularies,* i. no. 361.
61. *Ibid,* nos. 361n, 362, 363
62. See B. R. Kemp, 'The monastic dean of Leominster', *English Historical Review*, lxxxiii (1968), 505-15.
63. Below, p. 45.
64. *The Heads of Religious Houses: England and Wales, II, 1216-1377*, ed. D. M. Smith and V. C. M. London, (Cambridge, 2001), 117.
65. *Taxatio Ecclesiastica Angliae et Walliae auctoritate P. Nicholai IV,* ed. J. Caley, (Record Commission, 1802), 173.
66. Below, p. 49.

known, Reading Abbey, though originally settled with Cluniac Benedictine monks, was increasingly regarded from the second quarter of the 13th century as a simple Benedictine house, if I may so express it, and, as such participated in the regular meetings, or chapters, of the heads of the order ordered by pope Innocent III in 1215.[67] The 1277 annal shows that Reading was by then so much regarded as belonging with other Benedictine houses that the chapter itself was held there in that year. Furthermore, the annal alludes to the beginning of the process of setting up a Benedictine house, or college, in Oxford, to which gifted monks of any Benedictine house in the province of Canterbury could go in order to study at the university, and it claims for the abbot of Reading a central role in starting that process. Among other things, the annal states that the abbot of Reading requested of the abbot of Gloucester that he should erect a building for scholars on his estate in Stockwell Street in Oxford, close to a building of the abbot of St Albans, and that the request was granted, the abbot of St Albans agreeing to surrender part of his building to this end. Not all these details can probably be accepted without some qualification, but it is nevertheless clear that it was in this chapter at Reading that the decision was taken to establish a Benedictine college in Oxford for the use of the monks of any Benedictine house in the southern province of the order, a scheme brought to fruition in 1283 with the foundation of Gloucester College on the site now occupied by Worcester College, where by a delicious coincidence the manuscript containing these annals now resides. There is no reason to doubt that the abbot of Reading should have played so prominent a role; the abbot in question was Robert of Burgate, who was evidently keen on the education of his monks and appears to have been very interested in the arts, but who did not in the end exercise sufficient control over the abbey's finances and was required to resign from the abbacy in 1290.[68]

Finally, a few comments need to be made about the interpretation of dates in medieval English historical works and documents from the 13th century onwards, whether chronicles or annals – or indeed official documents and deeds. Although practice varied in earlier centuries, for most of the period covered by the second and third sets of these annals, and to some extent the first, the year was thought of as beginning on 25 March, so that any particular year did not end on 31 December, as we should now expect, but continued to the following 24 March, when it ended, and a new year began on 25 March. This means that an event occurring between 1 January and 24 March in any year by medieval dating would have to be dated a year later by modern reckoning - e. g., the flash of lightning which struck the abbey church on 12

67. For these chapters in England, see *Documents illustrating the Activities of the General and Provincial Chapters of the English Black Monks 1215-1540*, ed. W. A. Pantin, (3 vols, Camden Third Series, xlv, xlvii, liv, 1931-7); the Reading annal is printed, vol. i, p. 59. For Gloucester College, see J. Campbell, ' Gloucester College', in *Benedictines in Oxford*, ed. H. Wansbrough and A. Marett-Crosby, (London, 1997), 37-47.
68. *Reading Cartularies,* i. 28. The abbey had fallen seriously into debt by February 1275 and was taken temporarily into the king's hands 1286-9. (*Ibid*, nos, 81-3, 92-3, 98-9).

March in 1208, according to both the second and third set of annals, did so in 1209 by modern dating.[69] For dates between 25 March and 31 December there is generally no difference between the medieval and the modern dating.[70] On another aspect of dating, day-dates were often given in the Middle Ages either in accordance with the ancient Roman calendar (with its kalends, nones and ides) or in relation to the feasts and saints' days of the Christian calendar, so that in interpreting such dates one needs to consult the relevant historical aids.

69. 'Annales Radingenses Posteriores', 401; below, p. 21.
70. A caveat is necessary here, however, since in the third set of annals the year date is sometimes miscalculated for events occurring abroad or otherwise distant from Reading.

Annals of Reading Abbey III

[*p. 10*][a]
Anno domini M.C.XCIX. Obiit[b] Rex Ric' [ante Pascham][c] telo confossus apud castrum Caluc', quod situm est in pago Lemonicino vi. id' Aprilis, et sepultus est apud Fontem Ebraudi iuxta patrem suum. Johannes comes frater eius de Norm(annia) London' veniens coronatus est in die Ascens(ionis), qui fuit vi. kl' Junii. / Et eodem anno assumptus est Hugo abbas Rading' ad regimen monasterii Cluniacensis; qui monach(alem) ordinem annos xiiii. strenue rexit, et edificia et cultum religionis et reddit(us) multimodis ampliavit, et statum domus in pluribus melioravit. Cui succ(essit) bone memorie Helyas camerar(ius), vir per omnia laudabilis, et domus dei amator precipuus, ornamentorum in domo dei adquisitor magnificus, conventus et ordinis pacis et religionis conservator assiduus.

M.CC. Apud Andei allata est manus sancti Jacobi cum pluribus reliquiis sanctorum, super quibus sacramento sollempniter et sponte prestito Ph(ilippus) rex Francie coram magnatibus utriusque regni promisit se regi Anglorum omnibus diebus vite sue sine malo ingenio pacem servaturum. Et ut futuris temporibus pax utrinque in perpetuum perseveraret, Ludovicus filius regis Francie assensu patris sui neptem regis Anglie, filiam scilicet regis Hyspanie, sibi copulavit in matrimonium, set rex Francie, fidei sue et omnium que promiserat cito oblitus, a pacto fraudulenter resilivit, Normanniam acriter infestare cepit, et ad bellum regem Anglie provocavit. / Eodem anno rex Johannes rediit in Angliam post festum sancti Michaelis, adducens secum uxorem nomine Sibillam filiam comitis Engol'; quam sequenti dominica proxima ante festum sancti Dionisii reginam coronari fecit. / Johannes rex Anglie dedit Ph(ilippo) regi Francie pro bono pacis xx^{ti} milia marcarum. Elyas abbas Rading' benedicitur.

M.CC.I. Baldewinus comes Flandrie Ierusalem proficiscitur.

a. *For a note on pagination,* *see p.7.*
b. *Ms Ø, the same symbol being used throughout for* Obiit *or* Obierunt.
c. *Bracketed words underlined in red.*

Annals of Reading Abbey III

AD 1199. King Richard died on 8 April,[71] before Easter, having been pierced by an arrow at the castle of Chalus,[72] which is situated in the land of the Limousin, and was buried at Fontevrault next to his father. His brother John, coming to London from Normandy, was crowned on Ascension Day, 27 May. In the same year Hugh, abbot of Reading, was appointed to the rule of the monastery of Cluny; he (had) ruled the monastery[73] with vigour for fourteen years, in many ways he enlarged the buildings and expanded the worship and income, and in several ways improved the state of the house. He was succeeded by Elias the chamberlain, of good memory, a man praiseworthy in all things, a particular lover of the house of God, who acquired magnificent ornaments for the house of God, an assiduous preserver of the peace and religion of the convent and the order.

1200. To Andelys[74] was brought the hand of St James with many relics of saints, on which Philip, king of France, swore an oath solemnly and willingly before the magnates of both kingdoms, promising that he would keep peace with the king of the English all the days of his life, without evil intent. And in order that in the future peace should be preserved on both sides, Louis, son of the king of France,[75] with his father's consent, was joined in marriage with the niece of the king of England, namely, the daughter of the king of Spain,[76] but the king of France, soon forgetting his oath and all that he had promised, deceitfully broke the agreement, began to attack Normandy fiercely and provoked the king to war. In the same year King John returned to England after Michaelmas, bringing with him as his wife Isabel, daughter of the count of Angoulême, whom on the next Sunday after the feast of St Denis he caused to be crowned.[77] John, king of England, gave to Philip, king of France, 20,000 marks for the sake of peace. Elias was blessed as abbot of Reading.

1201. Baldwin, count of Flanders, set out for Jerusalem.[78]

71. Actually 6 April.
72. Chalus-Chabrol. The king died as the result of an arrow wound in his left shoulder during the siege of the castle (J. Gillingham, *Richard the Lionheart*, London, 1978, 276-7).
73. Namely, Reading Abbey.
74. Les Andelys; the meeting took place at a traditional site between Gaillon and Les Andelys on Ascension Day, 18 May (Norgate, 73).
75. The future King Louis VIII of France, who, as Prince Louis, was to invade England in 1216.
76. Blanche of Castile, daughter of King Alfonso VIII of Castile and Eleanor, a sister of King John.
77. Isabel, daughter of Audemar, count of Angoulême, married John as his second wife on 24 August, and was crowned in Westminster Abbey on 8 October.
78. For this expedition, during the Fourth Crusade, see H. E. Mayer, trans. J. Gillingham, *The Crusades*, (2nd edn, Oxford, 1988), 198 ff.

M.CC.II. Rex Johannes et Willelmus de Rupibus [ad vincula sancti Petri][a] ceperunt Arturum comitem Britannie [et nepotem regis ante(..)],[b] G. de Lisenan, H. le Brun, Savaricum de Mall', nec evasit unus de CCC. militibus apud Mirabel.

M.CC.III. Willelmus episcopus Lincoln' et Gaufredus de Sancto David consecrantur. Urbs Constantinopol' a comite Flandrie et duce Venecie cum exercitibus eorum Ierusalem tendentibus expugnata est. / Summa tritici in Anglia comparatur xvi. sol', et sextarium vini iiii^{or} sol.

[*p. 11*]
M.CC.IIII. Obiit Alienora regina. Item Godefridus Winton' episcopus. Abbas Helias concessit Laurencio Burgeys ballivo ville edificare capellam in honorem Edmundi martiris, iuxta quam se fecit heremitam.

M.CC.V. Obiit bone memorie Hub(ertus) archiepiscopus Cant'. Johannes rex post redditum suum de Pictavia in auxilium guerre sue et recompensationem ab omnibus suis in Anglia, laicis, clericis et etiam viris religiosis, xiii^{am} partem accepit reddituum et catallorum.

M.CC.VI. Johannes legatus venit in Angliam. Celebratum fuit concilium apud Rading' iiii. n' Aprilis.

M.CC.VII. Post festum sancti Michaelis vi. n' Octobris natus fuit Henricus rex filius Johannis regis. / Episcopus Hereford' Egidius nomine capitulum Leom(inistrie) subito intravit totumque statum et domum subvertere et sibi subiugare temptavit.

a. *Interlined in red.*
b. *In margin and marked for insertion.*

1202. King John and William des Roches, on the feast of St Peter in Chains, seized Arthur, count of Brittany and nephew of the king, G(eoffrey) de Lusignan, H(ugh) le Brun and Savaric de Mall', and not one of 300 knights escaped at Mirebeau.[79]

1203. William, bishop of Lincoln, and Geoffrey, bishop of St Davids, were consecrated.[80] The city of Constantinople was attacked by the count of Flanders and the doge of Venice with their armies on the way to Jerusalem.[81] A load of wheat in England cost 16 shillings, and a sester of wine 4 shillings.

1204. Queen Eleanor died; also Godfrey, bishop of Winchester.[82] Abbot Elias allowed Laurence Burgeys, bailiff of the town, to build a chapel in honour of Edmund the Martyr, next to which he made himself a hermit.[83]

1205. Hubert, archbishop of Canterbury, of good memory, died.[84] After his return from Poitou King John, in aid of his war and payment of his expenses, took from all the laity, clergy and even religious in England a thirteenth part of their rents and chattels.[85]

1206. The legate, John, came to England.[86] A council was held at Reading on 2 April.[87]

1207. After Michaelmas, on 2 October, King Henry, son of King John, was born[88] The bishop of Hereford, Giles by name,[89] suddenly entered the chapter of Leominster and attempted to change the whole establishment of the house and subjugate it to himself.

79. Arthur, the son of John's elder brother Geoffrey (d. 1186), was seized at Mirebeau on 1 August
80. William of Blois, bishop of Lincoln, and Geoffrey of Henlow, bishop of St Davids, were consecrated, respectively, on 24 August and 7 December.
81. For the crusaders' attack on Constantinople, beginning in April 1204, see Mayer, *Crusades*, 201-3.
82. Eleanor of Aquitaine, widow of Henry II, died 1 April; Godfrey de Lucy, bishop of Winchester, on 11 or 12 September.
83. See above, p. 10; BL, Cotton ms Vespasian Ev, fo. 81v.
84. Hubert Walter, archbishop of Canterbury, died July.
85. This annal is confused: John's expedition to Poitou took place in the summer of 1206, from which John returned to England in December; an assembly was held in London on 8 January 1207, from which the notorious 'thirteenth' eventually emanated on 9 February (S. Painter, *The Reign of King John*, (Baltimore, 1949), 131-2).
86. The legate of Pope Innocent III was John of Ferentino, cardinal deacon of S. Maria in Via lata.
87. The legatine council at Reading was actually held 18-20 October (*Councils and Synods*, II (i), 4-5); the legate is first recorded in England at Reading on 28 May (*PL*, ccxv. 792), but the date in the Reading annal may be related to the Southwark Annals, which say that he was in England from Easter (2 April in 1206) to Martinmas (11 November) (British Library, Cotton ms Faustina A viii, fo. 138r).
88. The future Henry III was actually born on 1 October.
89. Giles de Braose, bishop of Hereford, 1200-1215.

Set turpem repulsam passus vix inducias pacis reformande ad honestatem reg(is) et regni et Rading' ecclesie die accepto optinuit. Unde beatum illius loci advocatum apostolum Petrum satis offendit, sicut patenter claruit. Nam pene omnes qui ei assensum prebuerunt sensum at facultatem nocendi amiserunt, vel carcare sive exilio diu fatigati, extraneos divitiarum suarum dominos reliquerunt. Episcopus Hereford' Normann(iam) ut exulatus adiit, ubi marsupium usque ad sanguinem emunxit. Pater eius cum uxore et filiis Hyberniam nudus petiit. / Stephanus de Langet(on) apud Romam consecratus archiepiscopus Cant'. Et monachi Cant', expulsi de domo sua, exierunt ab Anglia. / Otto in cena domini applicuit in Angliam, pro quo ut dicitur xiiii^{ma} pars, sive xiii^{ma} mobilium et immobilium tocius Anglie fiscatur.

M.CC.VIII. Tenebrosus turbo totam ecclesiam Rading' vallavit. Deinde cecidit subito fulgur, et circumvolavit secundo turrim ecclesie, ceciditque et accendit prius aquilonarem partem ecclesie, et postea meridianam, in die sancti Gregorii. / Interdicta est Anglia generaliter ab omni ecclesiastico officio ab Innocentio papa ix. kl' Aprilis, duravitque per vi. annos et xiii. septimanas. Proscribuntur episcopi London', Elyens', Wygorn', interdicti prolatores. / Willelmus de Braosa exheredatus est.

M.CC.IX. Dux Saxonicus Henricus cum filio venit in Angliam. Predicti episcopi, videlicet executores cause archiepiscopi, in Angliam venerunt, regemque apud [*p. 12*] Norhant' adierunt, set sine effectu reversi sunt. Deinde post festum sancti Michaelis, a rege accersiti apud Doveram, cum archiepiscopo iterum applicuerunt; quibus rex occurrit, set rex leugis interpositis substitit et archiepiscopum per internuntios salutavit, eumque suis xeniis[a] honoravit. Set sequenti nocte ministri Belial regem corruperunt, et sic singuli ad sua sunt reversi. / Otto Rome ungitur in imperatorem iiii. n' Octobris. /

a. Ms xseniis.

He received an ignominious rebuff, however, and just managed to achieve a truce by accepting a date for restoring peace to the honour of the king and kingdom and of the church of Reading. Whereby, he grievously offended the blessed advocate of that place, the apostle Peter, as became very clear. For almost all those who gave him assent lost sense and power to hurt, being condemned to prison or exile, and left their riches to foreign lords. The bishop of Hereford went as an exile to Normandy, where he spent his last penny. His father,[90] with his wife and sons, made for Ireland destitute. Stephen Langton was consecrated archbishop of Canterbury at Rome,[91] and the monks of Canterbury were expelled from their house and left England. On Maundy Thursday (8 March) Otto[92] landed in England, for whom a fourteenth or thirteenth part of movables and immovables of the whole of England is said to have been levied.

1208. On St Gregory's day [12 March] a dark whirlwind swept round the entire church of Reading; then came a sudden flash of lightning, which flew round the tower of the church and descended and burnt first the north side of the church and afterwards the south. A general interdict of all ecclesiastical offices was imposed on England by Pope Innocent [III] on 24 March, which lasted for six years and thirteen weeks. The bishops of London, Ely and Worcester, who published the interdict,[93] went into exile. William de Braose was disinherited.[94]

1209. Henry, duke of Saxony, with his son came to England.[95] The said bishops, that is, the executors of the cause of the archbishop,[96] came to England and met the king at Northampton, but they returned without achieving anything.[97] Then after Michaelmas, summoned by the king at Dover, they landed again with the archbishop; the king met them, but stopped with six leagues between them and greeted the archbishop by intermediaries and honoured him with his gifts.[98] The following night, however, the ministers of Belial seduced the king, and so all went back to their homes. Otto was anointed as emperor in Rome on 4 October.[99]

90. William de Braose (d. 1211).
91. On 17 June.
92. Nephew of King John and emperor-elect of the Holy Roman Empire; he met King John in London in May (Norgate, 165-6).
93. Respectively, William of Sainte-Mère-Eglise; Eustace; Mauger.
94. On John's treatment of William de Braose at this juncture, see Norgate, 149-50.
95. This is probably an error for Henry, count palatine of the Rhine, son of Henry the Lion, duke of Saxony, and brother of Otto (see note 92), who is known to have visited England in 1209 (Matthew Paris, *Chronica Majora* ii. 524; Poole, 451).
96. See note 93.
97. Cf. F. M. Powicke, *Stephen Langton*, (Oxford, 1928), 77.
98. *Ibid.*
99 He was anointed and crowned as Emperor Otto IV. Other sources date this event to 21 October.

Johannes rex Anglorum perrexit contra regem Scottorum cum xxx. milibus armatorum. Cui rex Scottorum apud Berewyk pacifice occurrit, et quem pacificare ratione non potuit xv. milibus li(brorum) sterlingorum sibi pacificavit. / Natus est Ricardus filius Johannis regis viii. idus Januarii.

M.CC.X. Hoc anno rex Angl(ie) Johannes totam terram suam tam gravi exactione peccunie[a] fatigavit, ut etiam religiosos multos a suis sedibus expelleret, ceteris omnibus vix spem respirandi relinqueret. Deinde Hyberniam adiit, et Walterum de Laci eiecit, Hugonem de Laci pene nudum et expoliatum fugavit, regnum pacificavit. Matildem de Braosa cum primogenito suo a patria illa exterminavit. Quam prosequentes nuncii regis ceperunt et, regi pecunia mediante, restituerunt. Rex autem prius apud Bristoll'[b] nimis afflixit, et postea Wyndelesor' fame extinxit. Willelmus de Braosa transit in Normanniam, cuius uxor et filius apud Wyndelesor' in vinculis moriuntur. / Lata est sententia in Ottonem imperatorem. / Nata est Johanni regi filia, nomine Johanna.

M.CC.XI. Pandulfus nuntius domini pape venit in Angliam, et infecto negotio rediit. / Gaufredus de Norwyc' capitur apud Norhant', et inde ducitur apud Bristoll' et incarceratur. Johannes rex Walliam intravit usque Snaudune, et Lewelin(um) regem Walensium optinuit.

M.CC.XII. Orta est[c] discordia inter Johannem regem Angl(ie) et barones apud Notingeh(am). / Alexander filius regis Scocie indutus est novis armis apud Londoniam. / Obiit Adam prior Rading'. Eodem anno factus est conflictus inter Cristianos et Sarracenos in Yspania,

a. *Sic.*
b. *Of this word* sto *interlined in ms.*
c. *Interlined.*

John, king of the English, set out against the king of the Scots[100] with thirty thousand armed men. The king of Scots met him peacefully at Berwick and, being unable to placate him by reason, did so by £15000 sterling.[101] Richard, son of King John,[102] was born on 6 January.[103]

1210. This year John, king of England, harassed the whole of his land with such a heavy exaction of money that he expelled even many religious from their seats, scarcely leaving the others the hope of drawing breath. Then he went to Ireland[104] and ejected Walter de Lacy, pursued Hugh de Lacy[105] almost barefoot and naked, and pacified the kingdom. Matilda de Braose with her firstborn son he exiled, but the king's messengers pursued and took her and restored her after she had made an offering to the king. The king had, however, treated them very badly at Bristol, and afterwards starved them to death at Windsor.[106] William de Braose crossed over to Normandy,[107] while his wife and son were dying in chains at Windsor. Sentence was passed on the Emperor Otto.[108]A daughter named Joan was born to King John.[109]

1211. Pandulf the pope's nuncio came to England and returned without achieving his business.[110] Geoffrey of Norwich was captured at Northampton, taken thence to Bristol and imprisoned.[111] John invaded Wales as far as Snowdon,[112] and received Llewelyn,[113] king of the Welsh.

1212. Discord broke out between John, king of England, and the barons at Nottingham.[114] Alexander, son of the king of Scotland,[115] was given new arms at London.[116] Adam, prior of Reading, died. In the same year a conflict took place between the Christians and the Saracens in Spain, and as

100. William I, king of Scotland (1165-1214).
101. The meeting took place on 8 August, the amount of the payment being probably 15000 marks, but there is some uncertainty about the figure (see Poole, 282; Norgate, 133-4).
102. Future earl of Cornwall and King of the Romans.
103. Correctly 5 January.
104. He landed near Waterford on 20 June (Poole, 315).
105. For John's treatment of Walter de Lacy, lord of Meath, and his younger brother, Hugh de Lacy, lord of Ulster, see Norgate, 152; Poole, 315.
106. See Norgate, 156, 288.
107. Warren, 187.
108. Otto IV was excommunicated and deposed by Pope Innocent III on 18 November 1210.
109. 22 July; she married King Alexander II of Scotland in 1221.
110. The intention of the visit, which began in June or July, was to effect a reconciliation between the king and the clergy in England, which failed. (Norgate, 160-2).
111. Virtually everything in this annal is confused and uncertain, as the story is in most other chronicles that mention it (see, e.g., Warren, 12-13; Painter, 270-2; Poole, 427, n. 1).
112. Norgate, 158-9.
113. Llewelyn ap Iorwerth, Prince of Gwynedd (North Wales).
114. Norgate, 169.
115. The son of William I of Scotland and future King Alexander II of Scotland (1214- 49).
116. At Clerkenwell on 4 March (Norgate, 162).

et Sarraceni occisi sunt usque ad ix. milia hominum.

M.CC.XIII. Obiit Helyas abbas Rad'[a] xii. kl' Aug(usti). Cui successit Symon abbas Rading' ii. kl' Aug(usti). / Johannes rex iter arripuit versus Pictaviam. Item Nicholaus Tuscul', agens legationem suam per Angliam tempore generalis interdicti, ipsum interdictum relaxa[*p. 13*]vit in crastino sanctorum Processi et Martin(iani). Stephanus archiepiscopus receptus fuit a rege Johanne in Angliam. Item prostratum est castrum Bainardi in crastino sancti Hyllar(ii). / Obiit Gaufredus de Norwyc' in carcere apud Bristoll'. Item obiit Gaufredus filius Petri.

M.CC.XIIII. Vi. n' Julii relaxatum est interdictum in crastino Processi et Martin(iani), quod duraverat per annos vi. et menses iii. / Obiit Willelmus rex Scocie, cui successit Alexander filius eius. / Symon abbas Rading' in Franciam proficiscitur ad comitem Sar' inprisonatum. In recessu suo periit navis eius apud Witsond' cum magna parte hernesii sui, et submersi sunt vi. pueri de familia sua, aliis vix liberatis.

M.CC.XV. Obiit Eustachius Elyensis episcopus. / Barones Anglie diffidabant Johannem regem apud Rading' per Gaufr(edum) canonic(um) et capellanum Roberti filii Walteri convocant(is) et congregant(is) complices et coniuratos suos circa festum sancti Jacobi apud Norhamt'. De Norhamt' accesserunt London'. Die dominica summo mane intrabant civitatem acclamantes signum Roberti filii W(alteri), qui se gerebat marescallum exercitus dei et ecclesie. / Celebrata est universalis synodus Rom(e) presidente Innocentio papa iii; in qua fuerunt patriarchi ii, archiepiscopi, episcopi cccc, abbates dcccc. / Symon abbas Rading' versus Romam

a. Interlined.

many as 9,000 Saracen men were killed.[117]

1213. Elias, abbot of Reading, died on 21 July, and he was succeeded by Simon as abbot of Reading on 31 July. King John set out for Poitou.[118] Item Nicholas of Tusculum,[119] exercising his office as legate through England at the time of the general interdict, relaxed the interdict on the morrow of Saints Processus and Martinianus [i.e., 3 July].[120] Archbishop Stephen was received into England by King John.[121] Item Baynard's Castle was demolished the day after St Hilary [i.e., 14 January].[122] Geoffrey of Norwich died in prison at Bristol.[123] Item Geoffrey Fitz Peter died.[124]

1214. On 3rd July the interdict was relaxed on the morrow of Processus and Martinianus, having lasted for six years and three months.[125] William, king of Scotland, died,[126] and was succeeded by Alexander, his son. Simon, abbot of Reading, went to France to the imprisoned earl of Salisbury.[127] On his return his ship was lost at Wissant with a large part of his gear, and six of his household servants were drowned, the rest just managing to escape.[128]

1215. Eustace, bishop of Ely, died.[129] The barons of England defied King John at Reading by Geoffrey, canon and chaplain of Robert Fitz Walter, summoning and gathering his accomplices and conspirators at Northampton around the feast of St James [the Less, 1 May] at Northampton. From Northampton they went to London. On the Sunday, very early in the morning, they entered the city proclaiming the watchword of Robert Fitz Walter, who declared himself marshal of the army of God and the Church.[130] A universal synod was held in Rome[131] under the presidency of Pope Innocent III, which included two patriarchs, 400 archbishops and bishops, and 900 abbots. Abbot Simon of Reading crossed the Channel towards Rome

117. At the battle of Las Navas de Tolosa on 16 July, the Christians being led by King Alfonso VIII of Castile.
118. Originally planned for 1213, but postponed to 1214 (see Poole, 462-5).
119. Cardinal Nicholas de Romanis, bishop of Tusculum.
120. 2 July in some sources (see Norgate, 207, n. 2). The year is properly 1214, as in the following annal for that year.
121. 20 July1213, the archbishop, Stephen Langton, having arrived in England in June or July (Norgate, 186-7).
122. A stronghold of Robert Fitz Walter in London.
123. See above, n. 111.
124. Earl of Essex, died 14 October 1213.
125. See above, n. 120.
126. 4 December.
127. William Longespée.
128. For discussion, see above, pp. 10-11.
129. 3 February.
130. For discussion of this highly significant annal, see above, pp. 8-9.
131. The Fourth Lateran Council.

ad concilium transfretavit. Et fuit ibi a festo Omnium Sanctorum usque ad Cathedra sancti Petri.

M.CC.XVI. Ludovicus primogenitus regis Franc(ie) venit in Angliam; quem elegerunt barones in dominum Anglie. Et ex hoc oritur mortalis guerra per totam Angliam. / Obiit Innocentius papa iii. Cui successit Honorius. Item obiit Johannes apud Newerk', et sepultus apud Wygorn' in die sancti Luce. Cui successit Henricus filius eius. Et consecratus est in regem apud Glouc' in die apostolorum Symonis et Jude a domino Waltero de Gray Eborac' archiepiscopo et Petro Wynton', presente Guala sedis apostolice legato. Novem enim annorum erat cum regnare cepisset et unius mensis.

M.CC.XVII. Hoc anno fuit magna discunfetura apud Lincolniam sabbato in ebdomada Pentecost', xiii. kl' Junii. Et Franci qui convenerant ad succursum Lodowici, quidam in mari submersi sunt, quidam vero capti. Post hec cessavit guerra per Angliam.

[*p. 14*]

M.CC.XVIII. Dedicata est ecclesia Wygorn' a Silvestro eiusdem loci episcopo. Et translatio sancti Wlstani episcopi uno eodemque die, scilicet die jovis in ebdomada Pentecost', vii. idus Junii. / Dominus Gwala legatus recessit ab Anglia versus Romam. Et dominus Pandulfus successit eidem in legationem. / Rex Henricus sigillum proprium primo habuit per mandatum domini Honorii pape iii. / Obiit Romanorum imperator Otto circa Pascha. / W. Marescallus iunior, in recompensationem dampni quod fecit ecclesie Rading' tempore guerre, ad x. marcas annuas obligavit se donec melius et copiosius de terra vel de redditu ipsum locum respiceret.

on his way to the Council. And he was there from the feast of All Saints [1 November] to St Peter ad Cathedram [22 February].[132]

1216. Louis, the firstborn of the king of France, came to England[133] and was chosen by the barons as lord of England, from which arose a deadly war through the whole of England. Pope Innocent III died,[134] and was succeeded by Honorius [III].[135] King John died at Newark, and was buried at Worcester on St Luke's day [18 October].[136] He was succeeded by Henry, his son.[137] He was anointed king at Gloucester on the day of Saints Simon and Jude [28 October] by Walter de Gray, archbishop of York,[138] and Peter, [bishop] of Winchester,[139] in the presence of Guala, legate of the apostolic see, he being nine years and one month old when he began to reign.

1217. This year there was a great victory at Lincoln on the Saturday in the week of Pentecost, 20 May. And of the French who had assembled to support Louis, some were drowned in the sea,[140] but some were captured. After this the war ceased in England.

1218. The church of Worcester was dedicated by Silvester, the bishop thereof,[141] and the translation of St Wulfstan[142] the bishop took place on the very same day, namely, Thursday in the week of Pentecost, 7 June. Lord Guala,[143] the legate, left England for Rome, and Lord Pandulf[144] succeeded him in his legateship. King Henry first acquired his own seal by order of Pope Honorius III. Otto, emperor of the Romans, died around Easter (15 April).[145] W(illiam) Marshal, junior, in compensation for the damage he did to the church of Reading during the war, bound himself in ten marks annually until he could compensate the place in a better way and more copiously with land or rent.[146]

132. For discussion, see above, p. 11.
133. Prince Louis arrived on 21 May (Norgate, 268).
134. 16 July.
135. Elected on 18 July, crowned on 24 July.
136. John died on 18 October and was buried a few days later in Worcester cathedral.
137. King Henry III.
138. There is no other evidence that he took part (see *The Letters and Charters of Cardinal Guala Bicchieri, papal legate in England 1216-1218*, ed. N. Vincent, Canterbury and York Society, vol. 83 (1996), 28-9, no. 36).
139. Peter des Roches.
140. Referring to the sea fight off the coast of Sandwich, 24 August.
141. Silvester of Evesham., bishop of Worcester (d. 16 July 1218).
142. Bishop of Worcester 1062-95.
143. Cardinal Guala Bicchieri.
144. Pandulf Verracclo.
145. He died on 19 May.
146. See *Reading Cartularies*, ii. no. 1057, being William's deed as earl of Pembroke (1219-31), by which he gave to Reading Abbey 10 marks worth of land in Caversham, fulfilling this undertaking.

M.CC.XIX. Obiit Willelmus Marescallus senior pridie idus Maii apud Hailesb'. Item obiit Hugo de Mappenor' episcopus Hereford' apud Colewell', cui successit Hugo Foliot circa festum Omnium Sanctorum apud Cant'. / Civitas Damiete capitur a Cristianis die sancti Leonardi confessoris.

M.CC.XX. Prima coronatio regis Henrici iiii.[a] apud Westm' a domino Stephano Cantuar' archiepiscopo die Pent', videlicet xvi. kl' Junii. / Translatio sancti Thome archiepiscopi et martyris non' Julii anno l. post martyrium illius. / Ricardus episcopus Sar' videns ecclesiam suam in arto sitam, castro scilicet pene iunctam, transtulit eam ad Novam[b] Sar', ubi nunc fabrica ecclesie illius nobiliter constructa est, xvi. kl' Marcii, die scilicet sancti Valentini. / Inventum est corpus beati Augustini Anglorum episcopi apud Cant'. Item canonizatio sancti Hugonis Lincoln' episcopi auctoritate Honorii pape iii.

M.CC.XXI. Vivifica crux restituitur Cristianis et centum xxx. milia Cristianorum de captivitate Sarracenorum liberati, vigilia scilicet Decollationis beati Johannis Baptiste. Et propter hoc Damieta civitas ipsis Sarracenis reddita est. / Henricus rex Anglie dedit Alexandro regi Scocie J. sororem suam seniorem. Item Pandulfus electus Norwyc' cessit legationi sue ex mandato domini pape apud Westm'. / Isabella mater regis Anglie transfretavit, et nubens comiti Marchie inconsulto rege et eius consilio. Qui statim quedam castra regis Anglie in Pictavia expugnans occupavit. / W. Grubbe decanus Leom' factus est abbas Saloppesbirie.

a. *Sic.*
b. *Ms* Novum.

1219. William Marshal, senior, died on 14th May at *Hailesb'*.[147] Item Hugh de Mappenore, bishop of Hereford, died at Colwall [Herefs],[148] and was succeeded by Hugh Foliot around the feast of All Saints [1 November] at Canterbury.[149] The city of Damietta was captured by the Christians on the day of St Leonard the Confessor [6 November].[150]

1220. The first[151] coronation of King Henry III[152] at Westminster by lord Stephen, archbishop of Canterbury, on the day of Pentecost, that is, 17 May. Translation of St Thomas, archbishop and martyr, on 7th July in the fiftieth year after his martyrdom. Richard [Poore], bishop of Salisbury, seeing that his church was situated in a confined space, almost joined to the castle, transferred it to New Salisbury, where now the fabric of the church has been nobly built, on 14 February, that is, St Valentine's day.[153] The body of St Augustine, bishop of the English, was found at Canterbury.[154] Item the canonization of St Hugh, bishop of Lincoln, by authority of Pope Honorius III.[155]

1221. The life-giving Cross was restored to the Christians, and 130,000 Christians were liberated from Saracen captivity, on the eve of the Decollation of St John the Baptist [i. e., 28 August] on account of which the city of Damietta was returned to the Saracens.[156] Henry, king of England, gave his elder sister, Joan, to Alexander [II], king of Scotland.[157] Item Pandulf, bishop-elect of Norwich, resigned his legateship at Westminster by command of the lord pope.[158] Isabella,[159] mother of the king of England, crossed the sea and, without consulting the king and his council, married the count of La Marche,[160] who straightaway attacked and occupied certain of the king's castles in Poitou. W(alter) Grubbe, dean of Leominster, was made abbot of Shrewsbury.[161]

147. Earl of Pembroke; a hitherto unidentifiable place in Caversham.
148. He died on 16 April
149. He was consecrated on 27 October.
150. Mayer, *Crusades*, 225, giving the date as 5 November.
151. Actually the second, the first having been in 1216 (see above).
152. The original Latin calls him Henry IV, counting, as was common at this time, Henry II's eldest son, Henry the Young King, who was crowned in his father's lifetime, as Henry III.
153. The removal of the cathedral from Old Sarum to New Salisbury took place over several years; the process began in November 1219, but the foundation stones of the new building were laid on 28 April, 1220 (*EEA*, 18, *Salisbury 1087-1217*, lix-lx).
154. Not otherwise known; the tomb had been opened in 1091 and found not to contain the body, which had decomposed (D. Farmer, 'St Augustine's life and legacy', in *St Augustine's Abbey Canterbury*, ed. R. Gem (English Heritage, London, 1997), 26-7).
155. Hugh of Avalon (d. 1200) canonized 17 February.
156. Cf. Mayer, *Crusades*, 224.
157. They were married on 19 June.
158. In July.
159. Isabella of Angoulême, queen of King John.
160. Hugh de Lusignan.
161. Royal assent to his election was given on 23 July. His surname is not otherwise known.

M.CC.XXII. Cometa apparuit in occidente, tendens radium unum mire magnitudinis versus austrum. Et subsecutus est ventus [p. 15] magnus, arbores plures eradicans, turres et domos subvertens.

M.CC.XXIII. Obiit Philippus rex Francorum, qui regnavit annis xliiii^{or}, cui successit Ludovicus filius eius. / Orreum optimum apud Rading' consumptum est cum toto feno illius anni. / Eodem anno facta est exactio caruagii,[a] scilicet de singulis caruc(is) ii. sol'. Item rex H. ad deditionem compellit Lewelynum regem Walensium.

M.CC.XXIIII. Henricus rex obsedit castellum Bedeford'; nec destitit donec caperetur et everteretur, et eos qui intus erant laqueo suspenderet. Falconi data optione de tribus unum eligendi, scilicet ut perpetuo carcere teneretur, aut iuditio a magnatibus regni dato staret, vel a regno abdicatus perpetua proscriptione dampnaretur, elegit proscriptionem et expulsus est ab Anglia. Et Willelmus frater eius, cum aliis usque ad C. viros, suspendio punitus.

M.CC.XXV. Ricardus filius Johannis regis indutus est armis militaribus in die Purificationis apud Westm'. Et sequenti xl^{a} transfretavit in Gwascon(iam), et Willelmus comes Sar' avunculus eius et alii multi cum eo. Eodem anno facta est generalis exactio quindecime omnium mobilium et catallarum[b] per totam Angliam tam super viros ecclesiasticos et religiosos quam super seculares.

M.CC.XXVI. Obiit Lodovicus rex Franc(orum). Successit Lodovicus filius eius puer ix. annorum. Et obiit Willelmus comes Sar' et sepultus apud Novam Sarr'. / Item obiit Symon abbas Rading', cui successit dominus Adam de Latebir'.

a. Sic.
b. Sic.

1222. A comet appeared in the west, with an amazingly long tail stretching out to the south. And a great wind followed, uprooting many trees and overturning towers and houses.

1223. Philip [II], king of the French, died,[162] having reigned for forty-four years, and was succeeded by his son, Louis [VIII]. The finest barn at Reading was consumed by fire with all the hay of that year. In the same year a carucage was exacted, namely, from each plough 2 shillings. Item king Henry forced Llewelyn, king of the Welsh, to surrender.[163]

1224. King Henry besieged Bedford Castle,[164] and did not give up until he had captured and overthrown it, and those who were within were hanged by a noose. To Fawkes[165] was given three options to choose from, namely, to be held in perpetual imprisonment, or to stand by a sentence given by the magnates of the kingdom, or to be exiled from the realm and condemned to perpetual outlawry. He chose outlawry and was expelled from England. William, his brother, with as many as a hundred of his men, was punished by hanging.[166]

1225. Richard, son of King John,[167] was girt with military arms at Westminster on the day of the Purification [2 February] , and in the following Lent crossed over into Gascony, and William, earl of Salisbury,[168] his uncle, and many others with him. In the same year a general tax of a fifteenth of all movables and chattels was levied in the whole of England, both from ecclesiastics and religious and from the laity.

1226. Louis [VIII], king of France, died,[169] and was succeeded by his son, Louis [IX], a boy of nine years. And William, earl of Salisbury, died[170] and was buried at New Salisbury. Item Simon, abbot of Reading, died,[171] and was succeeded by lord Adam of Lathbury.

162. 14 July.
163. Under the leadership of Hubert de Burgh (Powicke, 394).
164. From 20 July to 15 August.
165. Fawkes de Breauté.
166. 15 August.
167. See note 102.
168. William Longespée.
169. 8 November.
170. 7 March.
171. 13 February

M.CC.XXVII. Obiit Honorius papa iii. Cui successit Gregorius, qui fuerat episcopus Hostiensis, tunc Hugo vocatus. / Eodem anno venit Ricardus comes Pictav' in Angliam de Gwascon'. Et in die Pent' accinxit eum Henricus rex frater suus ense cum comitatu Corbubie apud Westm'. Item Petrus episcopus Wint' iter arripuit versus terram sanctam ad festum sancti Johannis Baptiste. / Fredericus imperator excommunicatus est.

M.CC.XXVIII. Apud Sundonam obiit Stephanus archiepiscopus Cant', vii. idus Julii. / Gregorius papa ix. per Stephanum capellanum suum transmisit in Angliam omnium tam religiosorum quam secularium sibi vendicavit decimationem ecclesiarum ad guerram contra imperatorem conducendam et exercendam. Inponebatur enim ei quod concordiam fecerat cum paganis. Cito tamen concordati sunt dominus papa et imperator.

[*p. 16*]
M.CC.XXIX. Civitas Ierusalem reddita est Frederico imperatori, et in crastino ibidem coronam portavit sicut rex terre illius.

M.CC.XXX. Henricus rex transfretavit cum exercitu copioso ad recuperand(um) terras quas rex Francorum occupaverat, ubi viri magni nominis defuncti sunt. / Lewelinus princeps Wallie dolose ad se vocatum Willelmum de Braus' miserabiliter vitam finire fecit. / Eclypsis lune venit in nocte sancte Cecilie. / Obiit Ricardus Cant' archiepiscopus die Inventionis sancti Stephani. Post cuius mortem maximam difficultatem eligendi duravit per duos annos et amplius.

M.CC.XXXI. Obierunt[a] Willelmus Marescallus iunior et comes Glovernie in redditu eorum de partibus transmarinis.

M.CC.XXXII. Data quadragesima est omnium bonorum domino regi, tam a religiosis quam ab omnibus aliis per Angliam. / Hubertus de Burgo iustic(iarius)

a. Ms Ø.

1227. Pope Honorius III died,[172] and was succeeded by Gregory [IX],[173] who had been bishop of Ostia, then called Ugo. In the same year Richard, count of Poitou, came to England from Gascony, and on the day of Pentecost [30 May] King Henry, his brother, girt him with a sword with the county of Cornwall at Westminster. Item Peter, bishop of Winchester,[174] set out on his journey to the Holy Land at the feast of St John the Baptist [24 June].[175] The Emperor Frederick [II] was excommunicated.[176]

1228. At Slindon [Sussex] died Stephen, archbishop of Canterbury, on 9 July. Pope Gregory IX, through Stephen, his chaplain, sent to England for a tenth of the churches of all religious and seculars, which he claimed for himself to wage and execute the war against the emperor, who was accused of having made an agreement with the pagans. However, pope and emperor were soon reconciled.

1229. The city of Jerusalem was restored to Frederick, the emperor, and the next day he wore the crown as king of that land.[177]

1230. King Henry crossed the channel[178] with a well-equipped army to recover the lands which the king of the French had occupied, where famous men died. Llewelyn, prince of Wales, craftily called William de Braose to him and lamentably caused him to end his life.[179]An eclipse of the moon took place on the night of St Cecilia [22 November]. Richard [le Grant], archbishop of Canterbury, died on the day of the Invention of St Stephen [3 August],[180] after whose death the greatest difficulty of electing [a successor] lasted for two years and more.

1231. William Marshal, junior,[181] and the earl of Gloucester[182] died on their return from overseas.

1232. A fortieth of all goods was granted to the lord king, both by the religious and all others throughout England.[183] Hubert de Burgh, justiciar

172. 18 March.
173. Elected 19 March; crowned 21 March.
174. Peter des Roches.
175. He was to leave from Brindisi *c.* mid-August to join Frederick II's crusade (see *EEA* IX, *Winchester 1205-1238*, xxx and 158).
176. 29 September.
177. On the events of 17 and 18 March, see Mayer, *Crusades*, 237.
178. The king landed at Saint-Malo, 3 May, on his expedition to Brittany (Powicke, 94).
179. In April. (*Ibid*, 395).
180. He actually died in 1231.
181. Earl of Pembroke, died 6 April.
182. Gilbert de Clare, died 25 October 1230 (not 1231).
183. In September (Matthew Paris, *Chronica Majora*, iii. 155-6).

Anglie, captus est et incarceratus apud Divisas. / Fratres Minores[a] ab abbate et conventu Rading' quandam placiam optinuerunt apud Rading' in loco qui dicitur la Fastern', ubi domum ordinis sui postea construxerunt. / Flumen magnum et supra modum crescens, et inundaverunt aque per Kenetam et Lodonam. Et in vigilia Translationis sancti Benedicti subito advenit quod et diluvium a plerisque dicebatur.

M.CC.XXXIII. Hubertus de Burgo evasit de carcere per Gilebertum Basset et Ricardum Siward' cum aliis multis apud Divisas. / Depositus est Stephanus de Segrave de dignitate iustic(iarii), et post illum nullus fuit iustic(iarius), qui videbatur esse quasi secundus rex. / Obiit Hugo Lincoln' episcopus. Item Ricardus archiepiscopus Cant'. Cui successit magister Edmundus de Abend'. Item obierunt[b] Rand(ulfus) comes Cestrie, et Alanus Basset. Ricardus comes Cornubie duxit Ysab(ellam) relictam G. comitis Glouc', filiam W. Marescalli senioris. / Data est regi xl[a] pars omnium bonorum tocius regni. / Comes Britannie recessit a fidelitate regis Anglie. Obsessa est civitas Romana a Frederico imperatore propter discordiam motam inter dominum papam et cives Romanorum. / Fratres Minores venerunt Rading' ad habitand(um).

M.CC.XXXIIII. Magister Edmundus de Abendon' ad archiepiscopatum Cant' consecratus est, dominica scilicet media xl[a]. / Ricardus Marescall' cognomento Strangboe wlneratus[c] fuit in Hybernia die sabbati proxima post medium xl[e] ad [*p. 17*] quoddam bellum factum in planicie de Kildar, et moriebatur plaga illa apud Kilkenni infra viii. dies, vigilia scilicet Palmarum. Cui successit Gilebertus frater suus. / Eodem

a. *Followed by a short erasure.*
b. *Ms Ø.*
c. *Sic.*

of England, was captured and imprisoned at Devizes.[184] The Friars Minor obtained from the abbot and convent of Reading a site at Reading, in a place which is called The Vastern, where they later built a house of their order.[185] An abnormally large flood arose, and the waters of the Kennet and Loddon oveflowed. And on the eve of St Benedict [i.e., 20 March] there came what was called by many a deluge.

1233. Hubert de Burgh escaped from prison with the help of Gilbert Basset and Richard Siward and many others at Devizes.[186] Stephen of Seagrave was dismissed from the office of justiciar,[187] after whom there was no justiciar, because he seemed to be like a second king. Hugh [of Wells], bishop of Lincoln, died.[188] Item Richard [le Grant], archbishop of Canterbury, died,[189] and was succeeded by Master Edmund of Abingdon. Ranulph [de Blundeville], earl of Chester, and Alan Basset died.[190] Richard, earl of Cornwall, married Isabella, widow of G(ilbert) [de Clare], earl of Gloucester, daughter of W(illiam) Marshal, senior.[191] The king was granted a fortieth of all goods of the whole kingdom. The count of Brittany[192] renounced fealty to the king of England.[193] The city of Rome was besieged by Frederick, the emperor, on account of the discord caused between the lord pope and the Roman citizens.[194] The Friars Minor came to live in Reading.[195]

1234. Master Edmund of Abingdon was consecrated to the archbishopric of Canterbury on the Sunday in the middle of Lent.[196] Richard Marshal, called Strongbow,[197] was wounded in Ireland on the Sunday after the middle of Lent at a battle fought in the plain of Kildare, and died from the blow at Kilkenny within eight days, that is, on the eve of Palm Sunday [i.e., 15 April].[198] He was succeeded by Gilbert, his brother.[199] In the same

184. Late in 1232.
185. The abbot and convent's charter to the Friars is actually dated 14 July 1233 (*Reading Cartularies*, ii. 1024).
186. See Powicke, 60.
187. c. 25 May 1234 (not 1233).
188. 7 February 1235 (not 1233).
189. 3 August 1231 (not 1233).
190. Respectively, 26 October 1232 (not 1233); uncertain, 1232-3.
191. 30 March 1231 (not 1233).
192. Peter of Dreux.
193. November 1234 (not 1233).
194. Actually in 1234.
195. See note 185.
196. 2 April.
197. Earl of Pembroke; this name Strongbow is usually applied to Richard de Clare, earl of Pembroke (1138-48).
198. See A. J. Otway-Ruthven, *A History of Medieval Ireland*, (2nd edn., London, 1980), 97.
199. Earl of Pembroke, 1234-41.

anno obiit Hugo Foliot episcopus Hereford', vii. idus Augusti. Cui successit Rad(ulfus) de Maidenest'

M.CC.XXXV. Isabella filia regis Johannis maritata est Frederico imperatori. Facta est concordia inter dominum papam et Rom'. / Gilebertus Maresc' accepit in uxorem sororem regis Scocie. Magister Robertus Grosseteste consecratus est in episcopum Lincoln' apud Rading', videlicet die sancti Botulfi. Et quidam Frater Predicator, Petrus nomine, in episcopum de Sancto Asapho. / Obiit Petrus filius Hereberti.

M.CC.XXXVI. Henricus rex Anglie duxit in uxorem Alienoram filiam comitis Provincie. / Obiit Willelmus de Bleys episcopus Wigorn'. Cui successit Walterus de Cantilupo, qui consecratus fuit a domino papa. / Concessa est tricesima pars mobilium et inmobilium regi.

M.CC.XXXVII. Legatus Otto venit in Angliam circa festum beate Marie Magd(alene), quem misit dominus papa ad instantiam et petitionem domini regis; qui magnum celebravit concilium in oct(avis) sancti Martini apud Lond'. Idem autem legatus, per triennium et eo amplius[a] in Anglia moram faciens, graviter oppressit ecclesiam Angl(ie), nunc hospitia exigendo, nunc procurationes, nunc provisiones. / [b]Symon de Monte Forti duxit A. comitissam de Penbrok' post votum castitatis.[b]

M.CC.XXXVIII. Obiit Adam abbas. Cui successit R. de Cycestr'. / Symon de Monte Forti contraxit matrimonium cum A. comitissa de Penbr' sorore regis post sollempne votum castitatis. Propter quod multi nobiles et Ricardus frater suus, dedignantes et maxima ira accensi, insurrexerunt in regem, quia eis videbatur quod rex magis dilexit honorem et promotionem

a. Ms aplius.
b-b. Deleted.

year Hugh Foliot, bishop of Hereford, died on 7th August, and was succeeded by Ralph of Maidstone.[200]

1235. Isabella, daughter of King John, was married to Frederick, the emperor.[201] Peace was made between the lord pope and Rome.[202] Gilbert Marshal took to wife the sister of the king of Scotland.[203] Master Robert Grosseteste was consecrated bishop of Lincoln at Reading, that is, on St Botolph's day [17 June], and a certain Friar Preacher, Peter by name, as bishop of St Asaph.[204] Peter fitz Herbert died.[205]

1236. Henry, king of England, married Eleanor, daughter of the count of Provence.[206] William of Blois, bishop of Worcester, died,[207] and was succeeded by Walter de Cantilupe,[208] who was consecrated by the lord pope. A thirtieth of movables and immovables was granted to the king.[209]

1237. The legate Otto[210] came to England around the feast of St Mary Magdalene [22 July], whom the lord pope sent at the instance and request of the lord king.[211] He held a great council in the octave of St Martin [11 November] at London.[212] However, the legate remained in England for more than three years and gravely oppressed the English Church, by demanding now lodgings, now procurations, now provisions. Simon de Montfort married E(leanor), countess of Pembroke, after [her] vow of chastity.[213]

1238. Abbot Adam died and was succeeded by R(ichard) of Chichester.[214] Simon de Montfort contracted marriage with E(leanor), countess of Pembroke, sister of the king,[215] after [her] solemn vow of chastity, on account of which many nobles and Richard, the king's brother, were outraged and extremely angry, and rose up against the king, because it seemed to them that the king preferred the honour and advancement of

200. Consecrated 12 November.
201. *c.* 11 June.
202. October 1234.
203. Margaret, daughter of William I of Scotland and sister of Alexander II, 1 August.
204. Usually called Hywel, or Hugh.
205. A benefactor of the abbey and probably buried there (*Reading Cartularies*, i, no. 516).
206. 20 January.
207. 17 or 18 August.
208. Elected 30 August; consecrated 3 May 1237.
209. January 1237.
210. Cardinal deacon of S. Nicola in Carcere.
211. See Powicke, 74.
212. *Annales Monastici* , i. 253).
213. This annal is deleted in ms; see annal under 1238.
214. Adam of Lathbury died 6 April; Richard was elected 12 April.
215. Sister of Henry III, widow of William Marshal, earl of Pembroke (d. 1231); she married Simon de Montfort 7 January 1238.

alienigenarum quam proprie sue gentis. / Tricesima omnium mobilium in Anglia concessa est regi, exceptis bonis ecclesiarum. / Johanna regina Scocie obiit apud Havering', et ad peticionem regis sepulta est apud Tarentam. / Frumentum sordidissimum exortum est in tota Anglia, unde secuta est karistia magna anno sequenti. / Edmundus Cantuar' archiepiscopus Rom' perrexit circa festum sancte Lucie contra monachos Roffenses et contra monachos Cant', et propter quandam discordiam inter ipsum et monachos suos inpetravit a domino papa ut posset construere ecclesiam [*p. 18*] canonicorum secularium in aliqua ecclesiarum ad eum pleno iure spectantium. Et incoavit novum opus apud Maidenest', set dominus rex illud impedivit.

M.CC.XXXIX.[a] Natus est regi Henrico filius et vocatur Edwardus. / Obiit Lewelinus princeps Wallie, xvi. kl' Februarii. Item obiit Isabella comitissa Glovern(ie). / Radulfus episcopus Hereford' contulit se ad ordinem Fratrum Minorum. Dominus papa excommunicavit Fredericum imperatorem propter multas causas. / Dedicate sunt multe ecclesie: ecclesia Abendon', Glovern', Sancti [Iacobi][b] de Bristoll', Persor', Wycumb', Leom'.

M.CC.XL. Dominus papa gravem exactionem ab ecclesia Anglicana exegit circa Pasch'. Apparuerunt comete due, set obscure. / Obierunt[c] multi magnates in regno Anglie, videlicet Willelmus comes Warenn', Johannes comes Lincoln', Edmundus archiepiscopus Cant'. / Nata est Margareta filia regis Henrici apud Westm(onasterium). / Petrus de Aqua Alba consecratus est in episcopum Hereford'. / Propter maximas et frequentes aquarum inundationes medietas pontis inter villam Rading' et Caversam pene dissoluta cecidit. / Obiit Lucas abbas Abendon'; successit Johannes de Blomevile eiusdem loci monachus. / Dominus papa gravem exactionem ab ecclesia Anglicana exegit et extorsit quanta extorquere potuit ad guerram tenendam inter ipsum et imperatorem.

a. *Change of ink; no further enrichments in red ink.*
b. *Supplied; see Annales Monastici*, i, 112.
c. *Ms* Ø.

foreigners over those of his own people. A thirtieth of all movables was granted to the king, except the goods of churches.[216] Joan, queen of Scotland, died at Havering (Essex),[217] and at the king's request was buried at Tarrant.[218] The wheat crop was of very poor quality throughout England, and there was consequently a great dearth in the following year. Edmund [of Abingdon], archbishop of Canterbury, set out for Rome around the feast of St Lucy [13 December] against the monks of Rochester and the monks of Canterbury; and on account of some discord between him and his monks he obtained from the lord pope permission to build a church of secular canons in any one of the churches belonging to him by right. And he began a new work at Maidstone, but the lord king prevented it.

1239. A son was born to King Henry and was called Edward.[219] Llywelyn, prince of Wales, died on 17 January.[220] Item Isabella, countess of Gloucester, died.[221] Ralph, bishop of Hereford, joined the Order of Friars Minor.[222] The lord pope excommunicated Frederick the emperor, for many reasons.[223] Many churches were dedicated: the church of Abingdon,[224] Gloucester, St [James's] Bristol,[225] Pershore, Winchcombe, Leominster.

1240. The lord pope demanded a heavy tax from the English church around Easter [i.e., *c.* 15 April].[226] Two comets appeared, but obscurely. Many magnates in the kingdom of England died, namely, William, Earl Warenne, John, earl of Lincoln, Edmund, archbishop of Canterbury.[227] Margaret, daughter of King Henry,[228] was born at Westminster. Peter de Aquablanca was consecrated bishop of Hereford.[229] Because of many frequent floods half the bridge between the vill of Reading and Caversham was almost destroyed and collapsed. Luke, abbot of Abingdon, died, and was succeeded by John de Blosmevile,[230] a monk of the same place. The lord pope exacted a heavy tax from the English church, and extorted as much as he could extort to maintain the war between himself and the emperor.[231]

216. Actually, January 1237 (cf. note 209).
217. Daughter of King John and wife of Alexander II of Scotland, died 5 March.
218. The Cistercian abbey of nuns in Dorset.
219. 147. The future Edward I, born 17-18 June.
220. Correctly 11 April 1240.
221. Widow of Gilbert de Clare, earl of Gloucester, she died 17 January 1240.
222. See *EEA*, 35, *Hereford 1234-1275*, xxxvi.
223. 20 March.
224. 23 October.
225. 18 October.
226. The demand was for a fifteenth, later refused by the English clergy.
227. Respectively, 27 May, 22 July, 16 November.
228. 29 September, later queen of Scotland.
229. 23 December.
230. Royal assent to his election, 28 February 1241.
231. See note 226.

Unde imperator moleste tulit, et regem et regnum Anglie per militem suum diffidavit. / Obierunt[a] episcopus Sancti Andree Willelmus et Walterus de Lacy. Item consecrata est ecclesia Sancti Pauli Lond', kl' Octobris, presentibus ix. episcopis et aliis magnatibus. / Obiit Walterus de Lacy.

M.CC.XLI. Dominus papa, volens congregare concilium generale apud Romam, mandavit omnibus legatis suis tam in Anglia quam in Francia cum quibusdam prelatis ut Rom' venissent. Et hoc audiens imperator, mittens naves et galiotas cum innumera multitudine armatorum contra eos, invaserunt omnes. Legatos omnes cum quibusdam prelatis ceperunt, quosdam submerserunt, alios occiderunt. Pauci vero ex tanta multitudine evaserunt. / Gil(ebertus) Maresc', extinctus in quodam torneamento, obiit. / Natus est Alexandro regi Scocie filius, ii. n' Septembris, qui nomen patris accepit. / Henricus rex Anglie consilio suorum Walliam intravit, et David principem et omnes qui cum eo erant sibi subiugavit. [*p. 19*]. Obierunt[b] Rog(erus) episcopus Lond', Gilebertus Basset, Gregorius papa. / Otto legatus recessit et obiit.

M.CC.XLII. Ricardus comes Corn(ubie) rediit de Ierl'. / Nata est Beatrix filia H. regis. Item rex Henricus transfretavit secundo in Wasc(oniam) post Pascha.

M.CC.XL.III. Ricardus comes Corn(ubie) duxit Scenchiam sororem Alien(ore) regine Anglie in uxorem. / Consecratus est papa Innocentius iiii^us^, xviii. kl' Julii.

M.CC.XL.IIII. W. de Ralegh' episcopus Norwic' translatus est in ep(iscopum) Wint'.

M.CC.XL.V. Natus est Edmundus filius regis Henrici. / Obiit Thomas decanus Leom(inistrie), die scilicet sancti Luce. Cui successit Hubertus.

a. Ms Ø.
b. Ms Ø.

The emperor was very annoyed at this, and defied the king and kingdom of England by his knight. William, bishop of St Andrews, and Walter de Lacy died.[232] Item the church of St Paul, London, was consecrated on 1st October, in the presence of nine bishops and other magnates. Walter de Lacy died.

1241. The lord pope,[233] wishing to assemble a great council at Rome, ordered all his legates, both in England and in France, with other prelates to come to Rome. Hearing this, the emperor sent ships and galleys with an innumerable force of armed men against them and attacked them all. They captured all the legates with certain of the prelates, they drowned some and others they killed. Only a few of such a crowd escaped. Gilbert Marshal was mortally wounded in a tournament and died.[234] A son was born to Alexander [II], king of Scotland, on 4 September, and was given his father's name.[235] Henry, king of England, with the advice of his men, invaded Wales and subjugated Prince David and all those who were with him.[236] Roger [Niger], bishop of London, Gilbert Basset, and Pope Gregory [IX] died.[237] The legate Otto departed and died.[238]

1242. Richard, earl of Cornwall, returned from Jerusalem.[239] Beatrice, the king's daughter, was born.[240] Item King Henry crossed over a second time to Gascony after Easter [20 April].

1243. Richard, earl of Cornwall, married Sanchia, sister of Eleanor, queen of England.[241] Pope Innocent IV was consecrated on 14 June.[242]

1244. W(illiam) de Raleigh, bishop of Norwich, was translated to the see of Winchester.[243]

1245. Edmund, son of King Henry, was born.[244] Thomas, dean of Leominster, died on St Lucy's day [13 December] and was succeeded by Hubert.

232. Respectively, 9 July 1238; early 1241 (A. J. Otway-Ruthven, *A History of Medieval Ireland*, (2nd edn., London, 1980), 100).
233. Gregory IX.
234. 27 June.
235. The future Alexander III of Scotland.
236. About 24 August; cf. *Annales Monastici*, i. 120.
237. Respectively, 29 September; ? *c.* 1 August; 22 August.
238. He left England after Christmas 1240 (*Annales Monastici*, i. 116; ii. 328), but did not die immediately, becoming bishop of Porto in 1244.
239. May 1242 (Mayer, *Crusades*, 257).
240. 25 June.
241. 23 November.
242. Correctly, c. 28 June.
243. *c.* 10 September.
244. 16 January.

M.CC.XL.VI. Obiit Robertus Sar'episcopus. Cui successit W. de Ebor(aco). Item obiit comes Walterus Maresc'.

M.CC.XL.VII. Translacio sancti Edmundi Cant'. Item hoc anno factum est escambium monete tempore regis Henrici. Eodem anno factus est terremotus in multis locis cis mare et citra.

M.CC.XL.VIII. [*Blank*]

M.CC.XL.IX. Capta est civitas Damiette a rege Francorum die sancte Trinitatis, scilicet iii. kl' Junii. / Eodem anno Anianus consecratus est in episcopum de Sancto Asapho apud Leom(inistriam), dominica scilicet proxima ante festum sancti Johannis Baptiste, quem conse[*p. 20*]cravit Walterus Wygorn' episcopus, presentibus de Sancto David et Bangor' episcopis, idus Junii, littera dominicali C.

M.CC.L. Obiit Fredericus imperator. Item W. de Ralee episcopus Wint'. Cui successit Ailmerus frater regis.

M.CC.LI. [*Blank*]

M.CC.LII. Die nat(alis) domini factus est miles rex Scoc(ie) apud Ebor(acum) a domino Anglorum, cuius filiam Margar(etam) nomine in crastino desponsavit.

M.CC.LIII. Obiit Ricardus de Wych episcopus Cycest'.

M.CC.LIIII. Hoc anno venit rex H. de Wasc(onia) ad natale. Edwardus filius eius duxit Alienoram sororem regis Hisp(anie) in uxorem. Dedit etiam H. rex Edwardo filio suo Gasc(oniam), Hybern(iam), Wall(iam) scilicet comitatum Cestr(ie). / Obiit Innocentius papa iiii.

1246. Robert [de Bingham], bishop of Salisbury, died,[245] and was succeeded by W(illiam) of York.[246] Item Earl Walter Marshal died.[247]

1247. The translation of St Edmund of Canterbury.[248] Item this year an exchange of the money was made in King Henry's time. This year an earthquake occurred in many places, this side of the sea and beyond.

1248. [*Blank*]

1249. The city of Damietta was captured by the king of the French on Trinity Sunday, that is, 30 May.[249] In the same year Anian was consecrated bishop of St Asaph at Leominster on the Sunday before the feast of St John the Baptist, and he was consecrated by Walter [Cantilupe], bishop of Worcester, in the presence of the bishops of St David's and Bangor, 13 June, Dominical Letter C.[250]

1250. The Emperor Frederick [II] died;[251] item W(illiam) de Raleigh, bishop of Winchester,[252] who was succeeded by Aymer, the king's brother [i.e., half-brother].[253]

1251. [*Blank.*]

1252. On Christmas Day the king of Scotland[254] was made a knight at York by the lord king of the English, whose daughter Margaret he married on the following day [26 December].

1253. Richard de Wyche, bishop of Chichester, died.[255]

1254. This year King Henry came from Gascony at Christmas. Edward, his son, married Eleanor, sister of the king of Spain.[256] Also King Henry gave Edward, his son, Gascony, Ireland and Wales, that is, the earldom of Chester.[257] Pope Innocent IV died.[258]

245. 2 or 3 November.
246. Elected 8 December; consecrated 14 July 1247.
247. 24 November 1245, earl of Pembroke.
248. 9 June at Pontigny.
249. The port was actually taken on 6 June.
250. Sunday before the feast (Nativity) of St John Baptist in 1249 was 20 June, not 13 June.
251. 13 December.
252. 1 September.
253. Elected 4 November 1250, consecrated 16 May 1260.
254. Alexander III.
255. 2 or 3 April.
256. Eleanor of Castile, half-sister of King Alfonso X of Castile, married between 13 and 31 August.
257. See Powicke, 118.
258. 7 December.

M.CC.LV. Facta est eclypsis lune et solis. Obiit Walterus Ebor(acensis) archiepiscopus. Item obiit Willelmus Ebor(aci) episcopus Sar'. Cui successit magister Egidius de Brudep' [*p. 21*] archidiaconus Berksir'. Item obiit Johannes abbas Abend'. Cui successit Willelmus de Neubir'. / Ricardus comes Corn(ubie) suscepit regnum Alem(annie). Eodem anno, videlicet iiii. kl' Octobris, Hubertus decanus Leom(inistrie) venit Rading'. In cuius adventu dedit ad camer(am) CCC. marcas, ad opus infirmorum CC. marcas, fratribus separatim circiter xxx. marcas. Acquietavit eciam coquinam de ix. li' vii. s' v. d' ob'. Dedit etiam infirmis fratribus i. marcam. Omnia ista fecit in illo adventu, exceptis DCCC. li' et xviii. li' datis prius conventui infra spacium x. annorum.

M.CC.LVI. [*Blank*]

M.CC.LVII. Generalis guerra in Wall(ia).

M.CC.LVIII. Magnum parleamentum apud Oxon' pro legibus Angl(ie) corrigendis. / Expulsio iiii. fratrum regis. Item maritata est Isabella de Clara marchis(o) de Monte Ferrato. / Obiit Edmundus de Lacy, pridie kl' Junii. / Dedicacio ecclesie Sar'.

M.CC.LIX. [*Blank*]

M.CC.LX. Obiit Warinus de Hocton ', iiii. id' Aprilis. Item Stephanus de Burgilun, xii. kl' Octobris. Item Willelmus de Wygem', x. kl' Junii.

[*p. 22*]
M.CC.LXI. Obiit Ricardus de Cicestr' abbas Rading', [a]xi. kl' Aprilis.[a] Cui successit Ricardus Banastr(e). Item obiit Ricardus de Sutton' precentor, vi. non' Maii. Item Robertus de Oxonia, xi. kl' Augusti. Item Johannes de Guldef', iii kl' Octobris. Item Johannes de Forns', xiiii. kl' Februarii. Item Johannes de

a-a. Interlined.

1255. There was an eclipse of the moon and of the sun. Walter [de Gray], archbishop of York, died.[259] Item William of York, bishop of Salisbury, died,[260] and was succeeded by Master Giles of Bridport, archdeacon of Berkshire.[261] Item John [de Blosmeville], abbot of Abingdon, died,[262] and was succeeded by William of Newbury.[263] Richard, earl of Cornwall, received the kingdom of Germany.[264] In the same year, on 28 September, Hubert, dean of Leominster, came to Reading; and on his arrival he gave to the chamber 300 marks, to the infirmary 200 marks, and to the monks individually about 30 marks. He also paid off £9 7s. 1½ d. of the kitchen's debt, and gave the infirm brethren 1 mark. All this he did when he arrived, apart from the £818 given previously to the convent over the space of ten years.

1256. [*Blank*]

1257. General war in Wales.[265]

1258. A great parliament at Oxford to reform the laws of England.[266] Expulsion of four of the king's brothers.[267] Item Isabella de Clare was married to the Marquis of Montferrat.[268] Edmund de Lacy died on 31 May.[269] Dedication of the church of Salisbury.[270]

1259. [*Blank*]

1260. Warin of ?Houghton [Conquest][271] died on 10 April. Item Stephen de Burgilun on 20 September. Item William of Wigmore on 23 May.

1261. Richard of Chichester, abbot of Reading, died on 22 March, and was succeeded by Richard Bannister.[272] Item Richard of Sutton, precentor, died on 2 May. Item Robert of Oxford on 22 July. Item John of Guildford on 29 September. Item John de Forns' on 19 January. Item John of

259. 1 May.
260. 31 January 1256.
261. Royal assent to election 15 April 1256; consecrated 11 March 1257.
262. 11 June 1256.
263. Royal assent to election 24 July 1256.
264. Elected King of the Romans 13 January 1257; crowned 17 May.
265. See Powicke, 400 ff.
266. June-July.
267. The king's half-brothers, Geoffrey and Guy de Lusignan, William de Valence and Aymer de Valence, bishop elect of Winchester.
268. June (*Annales Monastici*, i. 162).
269. Heir to the earldom of Lincoln, died 2 June.
270. 29 September.
271. The abbey held the manor of How End in Houghton Conquest (Beds).
272. Royal assent to his election 26 March, diocesan confirmation 1 April (*Reading Cartularies*, i. 28).

Wymundeh' apud Leom', vii. kl' Julii.

M.CC.LXII. Obiit Egidius episcopus Sar'. Cui successit Walterus de la Wyle. Item obiit Ricardus comes Glovern(ie). Item combuste sunt domus regis apud West' die mercurii post festum sancte Agathe virginis. / Comes Rogerus Maresc' et M. comitissa Lincoln' fecerunt escambium. Item obiit Walterus de Leom(inistria) apud Scoc', vi. kl' Marcii.

M.CC.LXIII. Barones expugnare ceperunt adversar(ios) regni circa festum sancti Johannis Baptiste. Et die apostolorum Petri et Pauli venerunt barones apud Rading' armati. Item obiit Rogerus de Waleby, iii. non' Novembris. Item Alanus de Andever', non' Januarii. Item Adam de Lauton', xv. kl' Marcii.

M.CC.LXIIII. Capta est[a] villa et castrum Norhamt(ona) per regem. Item Symon filius comitis Leyc(estrie), P. de Monte Forti et alii quamplurimi milites capti sunt ibidem in xl[a]. Item Judei London' occisi et depredati sunt per barones. Item castrum Roffense captum est per barones citra Pascha. Item factum est prelium apud Lewes die mercurii ante festum sancti Dunstani, ii. idus Maii, inter regem et barones. Et cessit victoria baronibus. Rex vero ductus est usque Lond' et dimissus apud Westm', rex Alemannie ad turrim Lond', Edwardus apud Dover', comes vero Warenn', W. de Valens', Guido frater eius, Hugo le Bigot abierunt de prelio in partibus transmarinis ex parte regis. Henricus de Hasting' similiter abiit de prelio ex parte baronum per evasionem. Plures Lond' conversi in fugam, et occisi per viam. Item obiit Henricus de Glovern(ia), xii. kl' Julii. Item Symon de Braggeham, ii. non' Augusti. Item Jurdanus de Othery, iiii. id' Septembris. Item Ricardus de Suthhampt(ona) apud Scoc', vii. id' Novembris.

a. *Interlined.*

Wymondham[273] at Leominster on 25 June.

1262. Giles, bishop of Salisbury, died,[274] and was succeeded by Walter de la Wyle.[275] Item Richard, earl of Gloucester, died.[276] Item the king's houses at Westminster were burnt on Wednesday after the feast of St Agatha the Virgin [i.e., 7 February ?1263]. Earl Roger Marshal[277] and M., countess of Lincoln,[278] made an exchange. Item Walter of Leominster died at ?Stoke Prior [Herefordshire][279] 24 February [*i.e.* 1263].

1263. The barons began to attack the enemies of the kingdom around the feast of St John the Baptist. And on the day of the apostles Peter and Paul [29 June] the barons came to Reading in arms.[280] Item Roger de Waleby died on 3 November. Item Alan of Andover on 5 January. Item Adam de Lauton' on 15 February.

1264. The town and castle of Northampton were captured by the king.[281] Item Simon, son of the earl of Leicester, P(eter) de Montfort and a large number of other knights were seized there in Lent. Item the Jews of London were killed and plundered by the barons.[282] Item Rochester castle was captured by the barons after Easter [20 April].[283] Item the Battle of Lewes between the king and the barons took place on Wednesday before the feast of St Dunstan [19 May], 14 May; and victory went to the barons. The king was brought to London and detained at Westminster, the king of Germany[284] was taken to the Tower of London, and Edward brought to Dover, while the Earl Warenne,[285] W(illiam) de Valence, Guy his brother, and Hugh Bigot went from the battle overseas on the king's side. Similarly Henry of Hastings escaped from the battle on the barons' side. Many Londoners turned to flight and were killed on the way. Item Henry of Gloucester died on 20 June. Item Simon de Braggeham on 4 August. Item Jordan of ?Othery[286] on 11 September. Item Richard of Southampton at ?Stoke Prior on 7 November.

273. Possibly either Leicestershire or Norfolk.
274. 13 December.
275. Consecrated 27 May 1263.
276. Richard de Clare, died prob. 15 July.
277. No Earl Roger Marshal is known; almost certainly an error, but for whom is unknown.
278. Margaret de Lacy, widow of (i) John de Lacy, earl of Lincoln (d. 1240) and (ii) Walter Marshal, earl of Pembroke (d. 1245).
279. A manor within the Leominster lordship.
280. See above, p. 9.
281. Chiefly by the Lord Edward on the king's behalf, 6-7 April (Powicke, 186).
282. *Ibid*, 184.
283. Actually on Good Friday, 18 April.
284. Richard, earl of Cornwall and king of the Romans.
285. John de Warenne, earl of Surrey.
286. ?Somerset.

[*No surviving annals for 1265-1275.*]

[*p. 3*][a]
M.CC.LXXVI. Translatio sancti Ricardi de Cycestria. Item obiit Radulfus de Walingef(ordia), viii. id' Maii. Item Ricardus de Bleber', iiii. kl' Octobris. Item Symon de Sulebir' apud Leom(inistriam), xii. kl' Novembris. Item Petrus de Bechamt' apud Leom(inistriam), xvii. kl' Februarii. [b]Anno quo supra venerabilis pater Radyng' impetravit ab abbate Glovernie quod posset edificare in Stowelstret pro scolaribus suis Oxon'.[b]

M.CC.LXXVII. Lewelinus fecit homagium regi Edwardo apud Lond'. Et rex dedit ei in uxorem neptem suam, filiam videlicet Symonis de Monte Forti. Item obiit Hugo de Lincoln', iii. id' Septembris. Item Philippus de Byenst', xiii. kl' Octobris. Item Rad(ulfus) de Herdewik, vii. kl' Novembris.[c]

[*Additional annal, inserted into an earlier chronological table, p. 2.*][d]
Anno gracie Millesimo CC.LXXVII, in crastino exaltacionis Sancte Crucis, venerabilibus patribus de Sancto Augustino et Glaston' abbatibus presidentibus in capitulo generali celebrato Radyng, xl^{a}v. abbatibus nostri ordinis personaliter presentibus, supplicavit et petiit venerabilis pater Radyng' a venerabili patre Glovernie quod posset edificare pro scolaribus suis super fundum suum Oxon' in venella vocata Stokwelstret ad edificium abbatis Sancti Albani, et concessem est. Et venerabilis pater de Sancto Albano aliquid sui iuris edificii, prout in edificacione patet manifeste, in plenari capitulo nobis ob reverenciam nostre supplicacionis contulit graciose.

[*p. 3, cont*]
M.CC.LXXVIII. Obiit Nicholaus de Leom(inistria), ii. id' Aprilis. Item Helyas de Sottesbr', v. kl' Junii. Item Ranulfus de Andever' diac(onus), ii. id' Septembris.

M.CC.LXXIX. Innumerabiles Judei suspensi sunt propter tonsuram monete. Unde rex Edwardus precepit fieri novam monetam. Item obiit Robertus de Fikeldene, vii. id' Junii. Item Thomas de Sancto Edmundo, non' Julii. Item Willelmus de Brochol', id' Septembris. Item Walterus de Fornset' apud Scoc', v. id' Novembris. Item Ricardus de Bissopest', xv. kl' Aprilis.

a. *See above, p. 7.*
b-b. *In a different hand.*
c. *Followed in ms by* J.
d. *This annal is printed in Documents illustrating the Activities of the General and Provincial Chapters of the English Black Monks 1215-1540, ed. W. A. Pantin, (3 vols., Camden Third Series xlv, xlvii, liv, 1931-7), i. 59.*

[*No surviving annals for 1265-1275.*]

1276. Translation of St Richard of Chichester.[287] Item Ralph of Wallingford died on 8 May. Item Richard of Blewbury on 28 September. Item Simon de Sulebir' at Leominster on 21 October. Item Peter de Bechamt' at Leominster on 16 January. In the above year the venerable father [abbot] of Reading obtained from the abbot of Gloucester permission to erect a building for his scholars in Stockwell Street, Oxford.[288]

1277. Llewelyn did homage to King Edward at London.[289] And the king gave him in wife his niece, namely, the daughter of Simon de Montfort.[290] Item Hugh of Lincoln died on 11 September. Item Philip de Byenst' on 19 September. Item Ralph of Hardwick[291] on 26 October.

[*Additional annal, inserted into an earlier chronological table, page 2*]
AD 1277. On the morrow of the Exaltation of the Holy Cross [i. e., 15 September], the venerable fathers the abbots of St Augustine's [Canterbury] and Glastonbury being the presidents in a general chapter held at Reading, and forty-five abbots of our order being personally present, the venerable father [abbot] of Reading requested and sought from the venerable father [abbot] of Gloucester permission to erect a building for his scholars on his estate in Oxford in the lane called Stockwell Street at the building of the abbot of St Albans, and it was granted. And the venerable father [abbot] of St Albans graciously granted us in full chapter his right in that part of the building clearly belonging to him, out of regard for our request.[292]

1278. Nicholas of Leominster died on 12 April. Item Elias of Shottesbrooke on 28 May. Item Ranulf of Andover, deacon, on 12 September.

1279. An innumerable number of Jews were hanged for money-clipping, and so King Edward ordered a new coinage to be made.[293] Item Robert of Figheldean [Wiltshire] died on 7 June. Item Thomas de St Edmund on 7 July. Item William de Brochol' on 13 September. Item Walter de Fornset' at ?Stoke Prior on 9 November. Item Richard of Bishopstone[294] on 18 March.

287. Either 17 May or 15 June (*Annales Monastici*, ii. 122, 387).
288. This annal belongs in the following year; see below, the additional annal under 1277.
289. Llewelyn ap Gruffudd, prince of Wales, did homage at Westminster (Powicke, 412).
290. Eleanor; they were married at Worcester, 13 October 1278 (*Ibid*, 413-4).
291. Which of the many places of this name in England is referred to here is uncertain.
292. For discussion of this annal, see above, p. 14.
293. See Powicke, 633.
294. ?Either Buckinghamshire or Wiltshire.

M.CC.LXXX. Obiit Adam de Hocton ' supprior. vi. kl' Decembris.

[*At the foot of this page, in a later hand (?13th-century), the following entry, out of chronological sequence, being an expansion of part of the annal for 1204 on p. 11 (see above, p.18 of this edition)*:]

M.CC.IIII. Abbas Helyas concessit Laurencio Burgeys balivo ville[a] Radyng' edificare capellam in honorem Edmundi martiris, iuxta quam se fecit heremitam, ad cuius sustentacionem promisit se daturum unam mancionem in Novo Vico post decessum cognati sui. Require copiam in loco cartarum inter cedulas. Vide in quarto folio sequente.[b]

[*p. 4*]
M.CC.LXXXI. Obiit Adelina Dispensar', filia Phil(ippi) Basset, iii. id' Aprilis. Item obiit Willelmus Adam de Harl', xvii. kl' Julii.

a. *Interlined.*
b. *Meaning p. 11.*

1280. Adam of Houghton,[295] sub-prior, died on 26 November.

[*The following at foot of this page, out of chronological sequence*]
A.D. 1204. Abbot Elias allowed Laurence Burgeys, bailiff of the town of Reading, to build a chapel in honour of Edmund the Martyr, next to which he made himself a hermit, and for its maintenance he promised to give a house in New Street after the death of his cousin. A copy is to be found in the place where the charters are kept, among the documents. See the fourth folio following.[296]

1281. Adelina Despenser, daughter of Philip Basset,[297] died on 11 April. Item William Adam of ?Earley on 15 June.

295. See note 271.
296. See above under 1204 in main sequence of annals; the meaning of the final sentence here is unclear.
297. Also called Alina, she married Hugh le Despenser (killed at the battle of Evesham, 1265).

The Miracles of the Hand of St James[1]

By far the most important of the many religious relics preserved at Reading Abbey in the middle ages was the Hand of St. James.[2] The early history of this relic and the circumstances of its arrival in Reading in the twelfth century are rather obscure and even less has been known about how the relic was used and what miracles or miraculous cures, if any, it worked. Hitherto, however, the existence of a manuscript account of miraculous cures resulting from devotion to St. James and his relic at Reading has gone largely unnoticed by scholars. This account forms part of a handsome early thirteenth-century volume now in the library of the Dean and Chapter of Gloucester, but perhaps deriving originally from Reading Abbey or its dependent priory at Leominster in Herefordshire.[3] Although it contains no specific reference to the monks' acquisition of the relic, there are clues as to when it came into their possession and, more importantly, the account contains a considerable amount of information concerning the type and extent of contemporary devotion to the relic, the means by which it was employed to invoke the apostle's power, and the kinds of illnesses which were cured thereby.

The manuscript account is clearly a fair copy written throughout in the same neat hand of *c.* 1200,[4] but no attempt seems to have been made to arrange the stories in any sort of order. Certainly there is no chronological or geographical arrangement. Twenty-eight miracles are described, all but two being miraculous cures. Many cannot be dated at all precisely, but thirteen (possibly fourteen) stories contain internal evidence which enables fairly limited dates to be supplied and one is actually dated to a particular year, 1127. This last is in fact the earliest of those miracles which can be dated, but it comes last in the manuscript. All the miracles for which dates can be obtained took place before the death of Henry II in 1189 and the general

1. I am grateful to the late Denis Bethell, formerly of University College Dublin, for much valuable assistance in the preparation of this edition and translation.
2. A late twelfth-century list of the relics at Reading is to be found in one of the abbey's cartularies, B(ritish) L(ibrary), Egerton ms 3031, fos. 6v-8r; printed by R. Baxter, *The Royal Abbey of Reading* (Woodbridge, 2016), 303-317.
3. Gloucester Cathredral Library, ms 1, fos. 171v-175v. I am grateful to the Dean and Chapter, who kindly allowed me to study the manuscript and have generously consented to the printing and translation of these miracle accounts. The volume was not listed as a Reading or Leominster manuscript by N. R. Ker, *Medieval Libraries of Great Britain*, 2nd edn (London 1964), but it is included as a Leominster manuscript in the supplement to the 2nd edn by A. G. Watson (London 1987), 44, and as a Reading manuscript in Coates, *English Medieval Books,* 154, no. 55. The fact that it came to Gloucester cathedral by gift of a Herefordshire squire in the seventeenth century encourages a supposition of Leominster connections, while the other saints' lives and miracles which make up the volume indicate that it belonged to an English house with strong Cluniac and West Country connections, which would fit Reading's or Leominster's position. At any rate, there can be no doubt that the original text of the miracles of St James derives from Reading.
4. This hand is very closely similar to the main hand of the abbey's cartulary, B. L., Egerton 3031.

impression to be derived from the stories is that they were collected together around 1190-1200. This would suggest that the surviving version was written shortly after the original compilation, and this is borne out by the apparent purity of the text and general absence of obviously corrupt passages.

There is a certain amount of scholarly disagreement regarding the abbey's acquisition of the Hand of St. James. The Reading Cartularies include the purported text of a charter by Henry I in which he gives the relic to the abbot and convent, instructing them to preserve it honourably and reverently in the abbey and stating that it has been brought to England from Germany by his daughter the Empress Matilda.[5] The text as it stands cannot be genuine, for the witness list is impossible, including as it does both Rannulf the Chancellor, who died in 1123, and Simon bishop of Worcester, who was not elected and consecrated until 1125, as well as Roger Bigod, the steward, who died in 1107, fourteen years before the foundation of Reading Abbey was begun. Some scholars have therefore dismissed the charter as a complete fabrication, but, even if one accepts such a point of view, it does not follow that the gift which it purports to record must also be regarded as an invention. It is quite possible that Henry I gave the Hand of St James to Reading without an accompanying written document. Support for this hypothesis comes in the early thirteenth century, some three quarters of a century later (by which time it had become far more general to accompany grants of many kinds with written confirmations), for then, sometime after 1204, King John gave Reading Abbey part of the skull of St. Philip without written confirmation of his gift - at least the monks did not see fit to keep a record of any charter the king may have issued.[6] The admitted fabrication of Henry I's purported charter to Reading, therefore, proves only that the king did not grant that particular charter, and it may indicate that he did not issue a charter at all, but as to his alleged gift of the Hand it proves nothing.

In 1966 Dr Hans Mayer, in an important paper, advanced the view that the Hand did not in fact come to Reading until the beginning of Henry II's

5. B. L., Egerton 3031, fo. 14r :-

Henricus rex Anglie et dux Normannie abbati et conventui de Rading(ia), salutem. Sciatis quod gloriosam manum sancti Iacobi apostoli quam Matill(is) filia mea imperatrix de Alemannia rediens michi dedit, ipsius petitione vobis transmitto et in perpetuum ecclesie de Rading(ia) dono. Quare vobis mando quod eam cum omni veneratione suscipiatis, et tam vos quam posteri vestri quantum honoris et reverentie potestis sicut dignum est tantis tanti apostoli reliquiis iugiter in ecclesia de Rading(ia) exhibere curetis. Testibus: Willelmo Cant(uariensi) archiepiscopo, Matille imperatrice filia mea, Simone Wigorn(ensi) episcopo, Rannulfo cancell(ario), Roberto de Sigillo, Brientio filio Com(itis), Rogero Bigot dapifero meo, Willelmo de Crevequer. Apud Port'.

The text is printed in *Reading Cartularies*, i. no. 5; and calendared in *Regesta Regum Anglo-Normannorum, II, 1100-1135*, ed. C. Johnson and H. A. Cronne (Oxford, 1956), no. 1448.

6. The king's gift is noted, B. L. Egerton 3031, fo. 7r, as follows:

'Iohannes rex Anglie dedit nobis caput Philippi apostoli venerandum, et nobis nundinas ipso die concessit habere.' King John's grant in 1205 of the annual fair on the feast of SS Philip and James the Less is *Reading Cartularies*, i. no. 49.

reign and he demonstrated convincingly that the cult of St. James at Reading began to develop at that time.[7] He did not deny that it was the Empress Matilda who brought the Hand from Germany to England in 1126 after the death of her first husband, the Emperor Henry V, but he regarded the story that at her request Henry I gave it to Reading as a fabrication of the second half of the twelfth century, when the popularity of the relic and the growth of the cult led the monks to manufacture a link between their possession of the Hand and their illustrious founder. He pointed out that the twelfth-century annals of Reading[8] note Matilda's return from Germany in 1126 but fail to mention any gift of the Hand, and he suggested that the notice in Matthew Paris that the Hand was restored to Reading in 1155[9] refers to what was in reality an original gift of the relic in that year, which, under the influence of the later twelfth-century myth, was represented as a restoration. Dr Mayer recognized, however, that these arguments are not conclusive. What he said about the annals is true enough, but the annals are thin and sketchy in the extreme and omit many important events which took place in the abbey's history before the date of their last entry (the death of Henry II in 1189) including the dedication of the abbey church by Thomas Becket in 1164 and, if one were to accept Dr Mayer's suggestion, the 'gift' of the Hand in 1155.[10] Clearly an argument from silence in the annals is insufficient, His interpretation of Matthew Paris is even more difficult to justify, for earlier in the same chronicle, under the year 1136, there is an entry recording that the Hand was removed from Reading by Henry, bishop of Winchester.[11] Of this Dr Mayer made no mention, but it helps to explain why there needed to be a restoration of the relic to the monks in 1155. The only medieval statement known to the present writer which supports Dr Mayer's view that the Hand came first to Reading in 1155 occurs in the Chronicle attributed to Peter of Ickham which was copied into the cartulary of Leominster Priory, the abbey's Herefordshire cell. This reads: *eodem anno* [*sc.* 1156] *delata fuit manus sancti Jacobi apud Redinges.*[12] However, this reference (at least in the form in which we have it) dates from the fourteenth century and is therefore far too late to be accepted without question.

Apart from this notice, medieval statements regarding the gift of the Hand to Reading attribute it to Henry I. The annals of Worcester report that it was

7. H. E. Mayer, 'Staufische Weltherrschaft? Zum Brief Heinrichs II. von England an Friedrich Barbarossa von 1157', *Festschrift Karl Pivec*, ed. A. Haidacher und H. E. Mayer (Innsbruck 1966), esp. 270-278.

8. 'Annales Radingenses', 9-12.

9. Matthew Paris, *Chronica Majora*, ii. 210.

10. Neither of the other two surviving sets of Reading Abbey annals notes the gift of the Hand of St James. They are: 'Annales Radingenses Posteriores, 1135-1264', 400-403; Oxford, Worcester College Library, ms 213, pp. 2-4 and 10-22, printed in the present volume.

11. Matthew Paris, *Chronica Majora*, ii. 164.

12. B. L., Cotton ms Domitian A iii (Leominster cartulary), fo. 31v. An identical statement occurs in *Eulogium Historiarum*, ed. F. S. Haydon, 3 vols (London, Rolls Series, 1858-63), iii, 68.

he who sent the Hand to Reading[13] and Roger of Howden, writing in the 1190s, even attributes the king's motive in founding the abbey to his devotion to the relic which he placed there.[14] In short, while there is a certain amount of evidence, admittedly not conclusive, to support the view that the relic was given by Henry I, there is little apart from the growth of the cult to support the contention that it did not arrive in the abbey for the first time until 1155. The evidence tends towards the conclusion that Henry I presented the Hand to his new abbey in or after 1126, possibly at this stage only as a temporary expedient and probably without an accompanying charter; that for some unknown reason it was removed from the abbey by Henry of Blois in 1136, i.e., not long after the original gift and at a time when his brother Stephen was king and possibly the abbacy was vacant[15] and that it was returned to the monks in 1155, perhaps because of the high regard in which it was held by Henry II, as is apparent in some of the miracle stories of the Gloucester manuscript. It is true, as Dr Mayer shows, that the cult of St. James began to develop at Reading in the early years of Henry II, rather than under Henry I or Stephen, but if, as is here suggested, the monks had earlier been in possession of the Hand for a very few years only, there would hardly have been time for such a cult to become established. The charter of Henry I discussed above was no doubt forged, like some other supposedly early Reading charters, some time in Henry II's reign,[16] but this was done simply to provide documentary evidence for the abbey's rightful claim to the Hand which had been given originally by Henry I. If one can trust the omission of *dei gratia* in the royal style, the forgery can be dated before 1173 and may therefore have been made at the time of the relic's return to the abbey in 1155, in order to forestall any other attempt to remove it.

The survival of the miracle stories is a happy accident of fortune, for without them next to nothing would be known about the relic in the twelfth century beyond the facts that it was at Reading and was greatly prized by the monks. Apart from direct information on contemporary devotion to the Hand, the stories also throw up a good deal of incidental evidence on other aspects of the age. All but two of the miracles were miraculous cures, but no. XV involved the miraculous shifting of timber which had previously resisted efforts to move it, and no. XXV describes the fatal vengeance taken by St. James on a man who failed properly to observe his feast day. Not all the miracles were worked specifically by the Hand, but apart from no. XXV, all

13. *Annales Monastici,* iv. 378. The date given is 1133.
14. Roger of Howden, *Chronica*, ed. W. Stubbs, 4 vols (London, Rolls Series, 1868-71), i, 181.
15. Abbot Anscher of Reading died on 27 January, 1135, and his successor, Edward, was not made abbot until after the funeral of Henry I in the abbey early in 1136 ('Annales Radingenses', 10). Henry of Blois, bishop of Winchester, was with his brother, King Stephen, at the time of the funeral (*Regesta Regum Anglo-Normannnorum, III, 1135-1154*, ed. H. A. Cronne and R. H. C. Davis (Oxford, 1968), no. 386.
16. See C. Johnson, 'Some Charters of Henry I', *Historical Essays in Honour of James Tait*, ed. T. G. Edwards and others (Manchester, 1933), 137-42; *Reading Cartularies*, i. 19-22.

were related directly or indirectly to the Hand or to Reading where it was kept.

This is not the place to embark upon a full analysis of the importance of the stories, but some points can usefully be made. The largest number of cures resulted from the drinking by the invalid of 'water of St. James', which, as nos. XIV and XV make clear, was water in which the reliquary containing the Hand had been dipped.[17] This remedy cured two cases of hectic fever complicated by throat tumour and quinsy (nos. V and VI), two cases of fever (nos. XXIV and XXIVa), one case of an internal tumour (no. XXVI), one of a mother dying from failure to give birth (no. XXI), and two cases of unspecified illness (nos. I and VII). The apostle's water was either administered at Reading or sent to the victims, one of whom insisted on taking it at her local church (no. VII). Water of St. James was used in a different way in four other miracles, and probably also in a fifth (nos. IX, X, XIV, XV, and probably VIII). In no. IX a head tumour was cured by signing the sufferer's head with the reliquary and binding it up with a linen cloth moistened with the apostle's water, while no, X resulted from bathing a withered arm with the water. In the two closely related miracles (nos. XIV, XV), a plague at Bucklebury ceased after the area had been sprinkled with water of St. James, and timber which was needed to erect a memorial of that miracle, but which could not be shifted by earthly agencies, was miraculously moved after the yoke of oxen, ropes, a cart and the timber had been sprinkled with some of the same water. The unpleasant case described in no. VIII of a girl's withered arm which had become attached to her abdomen, was cured by holding the reliquary containing the Hand over her arm and bathing it with water unspecified, which may have been water of St. James. Sight of the reliquary was effective in four cases, involving respectively unspecified plague, internal pain, crippled legs, and blindness resulting from failure to observe St. James's feast day (nos. IV, XI, XII, XVIII). A number of cures came about merely by the coming of the victims to the abbey to pray or offer a candle to the apostle, there being no indication that the Hand was directly involved at all. A woman suffering from dropsy (no. II), a dumb clerk (no. III), a spastic boy (no. XIII), a woman sick with fever (no. XVII), a girl with a withered left side (no. XX), and a young man with a broken arm (no. XXII) were all cured in this way. In the last but one of these (no.XX) the miracle was apparently worked by Christ. Even more easy were those cures which followed, usually immediately, the taking of a vow by the invalid to visit Reading. An abbot of Notley was cured of some kind of eye trouble in this way (no. XIX), as were a young man whose arm had broken (no. XXII), a crippled woman (no. XXIII - she was actually cured while on her journey to Reading), and a youth who was so close to death that his father made the vow

17. Compare the 'Water of St Thomas', which figured in several miraculous cures worked by St Thomas Becket and which was the very much watered-down blood of the martyr; see *Becket Materials*, ii. xxx.

for him (no. XXVII). The subsequent fate of the young man with the broken arm pointed a salutary warning at those who made a vow of this kind and after being healed failed to fulfil it, for he neglected to perform his vow and promptly broke his other arm. In five of the stories the sick or disabled person was advised in a vision (usually of St. James, but sometimes unspecified) to go to Reading for a cure, and in one instance the advice was transmitted by a vision to a third party.

An analysis of the regions from which people came to be cured reveals something of the geographical extent of the relic's cult. Eleven of the miracles concerned Berkshire folk, including monks of Reading Abbey, and it is probable that two others concerned people who at least had Berkshire connections (nos. XXI, XXIV). Of the remaining invalids, two came from Oxfordshire, two came from Buckinghamshire (including an abbot of Notley), one each came from Essex, Herefordshire, Suffolk, Surrey (a canon of Merton), Sussex (or Kent) and Wiltshire, and finally there were the sheriff of Surrey (*?rectius* Sussex), the young man accompanying Prince John to Ireland in 1185, and the keeper of hounds who came from somewhere in the north of England.

As well as preserving a record of the miracles, the stories also served as splendid propaganda pieces. The writer lost few opportunities of advertising Reading Abbey as a goal of pilgrimage and a source of miraculous healing power. Possession of a wonder-working relic meant increased income from the offerings of pilgrims and at various points the present miracle stories include rather unsubtle reminders of this form of good works. For example, we are told that the sheriff who was cured in no. I promised to give the abbey 20s. per annum for the rest of his life and that he afterwards added to this an annual payment in salt. In their concern to promote the interest of Reading and its sacred relic the stories show traces of a certain rivalry with other pilgrimage centres. In the lengthy account of miracle XX, for instance, St. James, appearing in a vision to an invalid at the shrine of St. Thomas Becket at Canterbury, declares that she will not be cured at Canterbury or anywhere else, but only at Reading; while in no. XI, again in a vision, St James tells a sick woman not to take her candle to Salisbury, as she had planned, but to Reading. Many of the stories contain quite horrific details of the illnesses or disabilities from which victims were suffering and one may perhaps detect here also another sign of the desire to advertise the relic's extraordinary powers - it is as though the writer were saying that, however awful and hopeless the affliction might seem, St. James could cure it.

The incidental information which can be gleaned from these accounts is considerable. As Dr Mayer has remarked, the Hand of St. James had no competitor for pilgrimages in England in the twelfth century before the canonization of Becket in 1173, and it is of the greatest interest to note in nos. XIV and XXVI that Henry II clearly valued its supernatural power so highly that he had it brought to him on at least two occasions, once because he did not care to venture upon the sea without its protective blessing. Miracle XI

reveals that one of the earls of Gloucester with his wife and other nobles came to Reading in order to see and venerate the relic. If it were not for no. XVIII we should not know that Gilbert Foliot, bishop of London (1163-87), translated the sacred Hand from its old reliquary to a new one. No. I adds a little to our knowledge of the shadowy sheriff who was healed at Reading, and no. XXV gives a slightly different version of the death of the count of Boulogne in 1173 from that in Ralph de Diceto.[18] The plagues in Reading and Bucklebury in the twelfth century (nos. IV and XIV) are otherwise unknown and the sequel to the miraculous quelling of the Bucklebury pestilence (no. XV) helps to explain two charters of Jocelin, bishop of Salisbury, which survive in the Reading cartularies and have hitherto been difficult to interpret.[19] The references to the milking of sheep (no. VIII) and to Henry II sending to a woman in labour certain gems and precious stones which were believed to possess helpful powers (no. XXI) are of great interest, not least because they are introduced in a completely incidental and casual fashion.

In this translation, the form and style of the original have been kept as far as was compatible with readable modern English, but no consistent attempt has been made to adhere to the medieval punctuation. Proper names have been translated except in the case of a few place names where no certain identification could be made. Wherever possible a date for each miracle has been added and where necessary explanatory notes have been supplied. No attempt has been made to identify the biblical and other quotations incorporated in the text.

Finally, there are six references to the common practice of sufferers bringing or sending wax candles to Reading in the hope of gaining a cure through the power of the saint (nos. VIII, XI, XVIII, XX, XXI, XXII). In one case (no. XX) the suppliant lit her candle on entering the abbey church, and in another (no. XXII) a man who had broken both his arms brought penitently to Reading a wax arm with a hand, almost certainly in the form of a candle.[20]

18. See note to miracle XXV below.

19. See note to miracle XV below.

20. In this connection we know of the sending in 1274 of wax candles of the measurement of Henry, seven-year-old son of King Edward I, to seven healing relics, including that of St James at Reading, during the boy's final illness at Guildford (Surrey); each candle was made of 2 pounds of wax ('The Wardrobe and Household of Henry, son of Edward I', ed. Hilda Johnstone, *Bulletin of the John Rylands Library*, vii (1922-3), 398 and note 1, 409). I owe this reference to the kindness of Dr Mary Alexander.

Miracles of the Hand of St James at Reading

Domino docente didicimus quia servus qui dominicam pecuniam sudario involuere et abscondere maluit quam in lucrum expendere non solum talentum amisit quod habuit verum etiam damnationis sententiam excepit.[21] Tante igitur tamquam metuende sententie periculum declinare cupientes, divine largitionis talentum quod meritis beati Iacobi percepimus vel alios percepisse cognovimus modis quibus possumus posteritati porrigendum censuimus, tum ut spes audientium ex auditu roboretur tum [fo. 171v] ut in glorioso apostolo suo Cristus glorificetur.

[**Miracle 1**] Quidam vicecomes de Surreia nomine Malgerus Malcuvenaunt Rading(iam) veniens, gravi infirmitate correptus est, qua invalescente iamiam ad portas mortis approprinquare videbatur. Desperans igitur et desperatus de salute corporis recuperanda, de anime sue cepit tractare remedio. Dissolutione sui corporis pene apparente, hoc sibi potius et salubrius expedire videbatur, si vel moriens seculo et seculi actibus pro posse renuntiaret et monachi habitum susciperet. Monachi autem Rading(ie) asciti et super hoc requisiti voluntati eius et petitioni iam satisfecissent nisi timerent ne exquestores palacii causa vicecomitatus sui in eos calumpniam devolverent, et regiam pecuniam quam non acceperant ab eis exigerent. Unde, abbatis sui absentia in dilationem petitionis allegata, hoc solum promiserunt quia si mortis articulum imminere cernerent ei ad succurrendum habitum patrarent. Sequenti vero nocte, cum iam in extremis laborare videretur, iterum sub magna festinatione vocati sunt monachi, ut vel morienti antequam ultimus a corpore solveretur spiritus habitum sicut promiserant prestarent. Nutu vero divino ampullam cum aqua qua beati Iacobi manus intincta fuerat monachi secum detulerant. Et licet de effectu virtutis apostolice imminente mortis periculo hesitarent, hesitationem pietate condientes, guttam aque salutaris ori eius infuderunt. Qui autem in area more morientium expositus prius iacuerat mortuo simillimus, contra spem omnium qui aderant stillam infusam transglutavit. Quod et secundo et tercio factum est. Mirabili dictu, sed mirabilius effectu, post trinam sancti liquoris degustationem membra recalescere, sanguis sese per artus diffundere, corpus emortuum cepit reviviscere. Unde de area sublatus, et in lecto suo recollocatus, in sudorem resolvitur et in soporem. Post unius vel duarum horarum spacium is qui

21. This passage refers to the the Parable of the Talents, recounted in Matth. 25: 14-30.

The Miracles of the Hand of St James at Reading

From the Lord's teaching we learn how the servant who preferred to wrap up his master's money in a cloth and bury it, rather than invest it for profit, not only lost the talent which he had, but also incurred a sentence of condemnation. Desiring, therefore, to avoid the danger of so frightful a sentence, we have thought fit to hand on to posterity, in what ways we can, the talent of divine bounty which we have received, or we know others have received, by the merits of the blessed James, so that not only the hopes of our hearers may be strengthened by what they hear, but also Christ may be glorified in his glorious apostle.

MIRACLE I (1155-56)

A certain sheriff of Surrey, named Mauger Malcuvenant, came to Reading in the grip of a serious illness. As it got worse he seemed to be drawing ever nearer to the gates of death. In despair, therefore, and without hope of recovering the health of his body, he began to take steps for the cure of his soul. As the break-up of his body was almost in sight, it seemed to him better and more beneficial if, even at death, he renounced the world and the ways of the world as far as possible and assumed the habit of a monk. The monks of Reading, when approached and asked about it, would have granted his wish and request, but they were afraid that the royal officials would transfer to them claims in respect of his shrievalty and demand from them royal revenue which they had not received. Accordingly they used their abbot's absence as an excuse for delaying an answer to his request and promised him only this, that, if they saw that the point of death was imminent, they would grant him the habit *ad succurendum.* That night, in fact, as he seemed to be in his final agony, the monks were again called in great haste in order that, even at death before the last breath left his body, they might give him the habit as they had promised. But, by divine will the monks had brought down with them an ampulla containing water in which the Hand of St. James had been dipped. And, although they were uncertain about the efficacy of the apostle's power when the danger of death was imminent, they seasoned their doubts with faith and poured a drop of the health-giving water into his mouth. He had previously been lying on the floor laid out in the manner of the dead and looking very much like a dead man, when, contrary to the expectation of all who were present, he swallowed the drop that had been poured. This happened a second and a third time and, wonderful to say, but more wonderful in its outcome, after this threefold taste of the sacred liquid, his limbs began to grow warm again, blood began to flow through his joints and his dead body began to revive. He was therefore lifted up from the floor and laid back on his bed, after which he began to sweat and fell asleep. After one or two hours he who had been

infirmatus fuerat, quasi de gravi sompno evigilans, de lecto surrexit et exiliens stetit. Qui vero convenerant et circumsederant ut viderent finem,[22] subitationem insperate salutis videntes et admirantes, loquebantur mutuo dicentes, 'Quidnam hoc vult esse?' Qui autem egrotaverat in vocem confessionis et exultationis erumpens ait, 'Deo gratias et sancto Iacobo, qui me vite et saluti restituit'. Virtus enim apostolica sibi apparuerat et in salutem perfectam erexerat. Omnibus itaque Deum collaudantibus, ipse solus nullo sustentante vel adminiculante cum illusceret ad ecclesiam devotus perrexit et quas debuit Deo et sancto Iacobo gratias retulit. Expletis missarum solempniis capitulum introivit, quomodo convaluerit ennaravit et ut in societatem conventus susciperetur obtinuit. Qui cum impetrasset, xx. solidos pro amore et honore beati apostoli qui eum a faucibus mortis abstraxerat conventui prebuit, et tantumdem pecunie singulis annis quoad viveret se eis daturum solempni voto promisit, quem voti sui affectum effectu complevit et succedente tempore devotionis sue munera ampliavit, quendam redditum salis annuatim exhibendo.

[**Miracle II**] Sub eodem fere tempore erat quedam mulier in villa que dicitur Erleia morbo tumefacta ydropico. Que de beati Iacobi confisa suffragiis venit in vigilia natalis eiusdem Rading(iam) Deum et beatum apostolum pro sua incommoditate deprecatura. Circa primam vigiliam noctis monachis matutinos inchoantibus, mulier prefata secus pavimentum presbiterii corruens cepit agitari et in salutem suam medullitus conturbari. Commota sunt quippe viscera eius. Decurso in hac anxietate aliquanto noctis spacio, ecce ventris eruperunt abissi et cataracte viscerum aperte sunt. Vomuit itaque et revomuit virus iamdiu conceptum, omnemque tabem noxii humoris exinanivit. Antequam diesceret, priusquam nox in suo cursu ultimum iter haberet, beati Iacobi clementia tantam habuit efficatiam ut venter mulieris zona propria pro admiratione cernentium quatuor palmis gracilior haberetur. Igitur in perfectam sanitatem roborata, ad gratiarum accenditur actiones. Turba multa

22. Cf. Matth. 26:58.

an invalid awoke as though from a deep sleep, sprang from his bed and stood up. Those who had gathered and sat down around him to see his end were amazed when they saw the speed of his unexpected cure and said to one another, 'What can this mean ?' And he who had been ill broke out in a voice of exulting faith, saying, 'Thanks be to God and to St. James, who has restored me to life and health'. For the apostle's power had appeared to him and had raised him up to perfect health. And so, as the day was dawning, with everyone praising God, he went devoutly to the church needing no support or prop from anyone and rendered due thanks to God and St. James. After mass he went into the chapter house and told how he had been healed, and his request that he might be received into confraternity with the convent was granted. And when he had obtained his wish, he offered to the convent 20 shillings for the love and honour of the blessed apostle who had snatched him from the jaws of death and he promised by a solemn oath to give them the same amount of money every year until he died. He fulfilled the object of his vow and as time passed he added to his devotional generosity by presenting annually a certain render of salt.

Note: Mauger Malcuvenant was sheriff of Sussex from Michaelmas 1155 to Michaelmas 1156 *(Pipe Roll 2 Henry II,* 60), but otherwise is unknown. Either the writer has misrepresented him as sheriff of Surrey (since, although later the two shires were held together, such was not the case in the twelfth century) or else he may possibly have acted as sheriff of Sussex during the reign of Stephen, for which the exchequer pipe rolls are lost. Apart from this story, there is no other evidence for Mauger's gifts in money and kind to the monks of Reading.

MIRACLE II (c. 1155)

At, about the same time a certain woman in the village of Earley became swollen with the disease of dropsy. Believing that the blessed James would help her, she came to Reading on the eve of his nativity to call in her affliction upon God and the blessed apostle. At about the first vigil of the night, just as the monks were beginning matins, the aforesaid woman threw herself on the pavement of the presbytery and began to writhe and to have her inside stirred up from the very marrow for the sake of her health. Indeed, her very bowels were stirred up. She had passed some part of the night in this agony, when suddenly the pits of her stomach burst forth and the flood-gates of her bowels were opened. Again and again, she vomited up the poison which she had built up over a long period and cleared out all the filth of harmful fluid. Before daybreak, before the night had run its full course, the mercy of the blessed James had been so efficacious that, when the woman's stomach was measured, to people's amazement it was found to be four handbreadths narrower than her own girdle. And so, restored to perfect health, she was eager to give thanks. The great crowd which had

que convenerat ad diem festum laudabant et glorificabant Deum in omnibus que audierant et viderant.

[**Miracle III**] Quam terribilis sit Dominus in consiliis super filios hominum Iohannis clerici testatur valitudo. Qui subito causa incognita loquendi amittens facultatem, aliquandiu mutus permansit. Qui predicta predicti apostoli solempnitate pro nature defectu nature supplicaturus auctori, Rading(iam) venit. Ubi dum vigiliarum lucubratione noctem orando protraheret, resolutum est vinculum lingue eius et loquebatur recte[23] magnificans Deum. Glorificatur exinde apud Berkingie incolas virtus apostolica qui prefatum Iohannem et mutum Radingiam proficiscentem noverant et in redeuntem loqui audierunt. Qui multis postea annis in capella abatisse et in hos[fo. 172r]pitio serviens quid sibi acciderit et quomodo convaluerit, in laudem apostoli crebro solitus est enarrare.

[**Miracle IV**] Multifarie multisque modis mirificavit Dominus sanctum suum. In Radingiis quondam pestis pessima et mortifera emergens, iuvenes et virgines, senes cum iunioribus prostravit, et filiabus pharetre sue populum non modicum vindemiavit. Quo tempore infra brevissimum anni spatium xiii. monachi de abbatia Radingensi de medio sublati sunt. Ceterorum autem quamplurimi de conventu plurimum infirmati sunt. Et cum non esset qui adiuvaret,[24] clamaverunt ad Dominum ut a gravissante periculo eos eriperet et procellam in auram statueret. Propensiore igitur habito delecto statutum est ut indicto ieiunio populoque ad ecclesiam congregato, speciales letanie fierent, et disposita generali processione villam circuirent, et per beati Iacobi patrocinia cuius manum efferebant Deum placare intenderent. Factumque est ita. In plateis autem ponebantur infirmi, in domorum autem limitibus emortui, ut capsam qua sacra manus continebatur aspicerent, et liberarentur ab infirmitatibus suis. Nam ut multi testantur, pene quicumque eam illa die videbant sani fiebant a quacumque detinebantur infirmitate,

23. Mark 7:35.
24. Ps. 22:11

gathered for the feast day praised and glorified God for all the things which they had heard and seen.

Note: Earley lay just outside Reading to the east.

MIRACLE III (*c.* 1155)

How fearful the Lord is in his purposes for the sons of men, the state of health of John the clerk bears witness. Suddenly and for some unknown reason he lost the power of speech and remained dumb for some long time. At the same celebration of the said apostle's feast, he came to Reading to entreat the creator of nature in respect of his own defect of nature. There, as he spent the night in prayer and carrying out of vigils, the chain of his tongue was loosed and he spoke normally, magnifying God. Afterwards the apostle's power was glorified by the inhabitants of Barking, for they knew that the aforesaid John had been dumb when he set out for Reading and yet on his return they heard him speak. And for many years afterwards in the abbess's chapel and in the guesthouse, where he was a servant, he used frequently to tell, in praise of the apostle, what happened to him and how he was healed.

Note: Barking, a house of Benedictine nuns re-founded in the tenth century had no particular connection with Reading.

MIRACLE IV

The Lord magnified his saint in many places and in many ways. In Reading there occurred at one time a disastrous and fatal plague which laid low young boys and girls as well as old folk and gathered a rich harvest of people with the daughters of its quiver.[25] And at that time, within the space of one short year, thirteen monks of Reading Abbey were carried off and, of the rest, very many of the convent were exceedingly ill. And, since there was nobody to help them, they called upon the Lord to rescue them from their growing danger and to send a strong wind through the air. Accordingly an important decision was taken and it was decreed that a fast be proclaimed and the people be congregated in the church, when special litanies would be sung and they would perambulate the town in a well-ordered general procession in the hope of placating God by the protection of the blessed James whose hand they bore aloft. And this was done. The sick were laid out in the streets (the dead being kept indoors), so that they might look upon the reliquary which contained the sacred hand and be delivered from their infirmities. And indeed, as many can witness, almost everyone who saw it on that day was made well, whatever the sickness from which they were suffering, because

25. i.e., Arrows. The phrase is borrowed from Lamentations, iii, 13.

quia virtus de illa exiebatur sanabat omnes. Eodem die, eadem hora, cessavit quassatio, sanata est populi contritio, placata est Domini indignatio. Omnibus igitur expletis, in sua quique leti redierunt, et ab illa die et deinceps ab huiusmodi pestilentia immunes extiterunt.

[**Miracle V**] Prelibato tempore quo populum suum Dominus vindemiaret filiabus pharetre sue filios suos decimaret, erat quidam homo Rading(ie) nomine Eadwardus, cognomento Haver, qui languore preventus vehementissime egrotare cepit, et maxime febre sinocha. Homine aliquandiu hac egritudine afflicto, supervenit egritudo egritudini, dolor dolori, squinantia febri. Que cum sint collactanee tunc urgent precipue, cum fuerint coniuncte. Miseri hominis miseros artus depascebat febris, alimentum vel refrigerium corpori denegebat vehemens constrictio gutturis. Eger nichil potuit reicere nec transglutire. Iamiam levis et modica videbatur angustia febris precedentis, respectu squinantie insequentis. Iam omnem escam abhominata est anima eius, et appropinquavit usque ad portas mortis. Aliquantis diebus in hoc dolore decursis, aquam beati Iacobi de monasterio monachorum Rading' sibi transmissam plenus fide ebibit, et contra spem incorporavit. Ilico tumor gutturis reprimitur, constrictio dissolvitur, vox pene interclusa reparatur, et sic salutari antidoto potus in sudorem resolvitur, et post pusillum plene saluti restituitur. Surrexit igitur sanus et incolumis et, quod diu non fecerat, manducavit et bibit, et Deo sanctoque Iacobo dignas et debitas gratias exsolvit.

[**Miracle VI**] Elapsis aliquot diebus, filia prefati viri in eandem in quam pater prius incidit egritudinem. Unde pater pro filia anxius, compulsus est recurrere ad illam quam ipse prius expertus fuerat medicinam. Predictam igitur predicti apostoli aquam postulatam impetravit et filie sue propinavit. Qua exhausta, que egrotaverat citissime convaluit et saluti restituta, una cum patre suo votiva oblationum libamina ad monasterium veniens sancto Iacobo persolvit.

power came forth from it and healed them all. On the same day and at the same hour the affliction ceased, the grief of the people was allayed, and the indignation of the Lord appeased. So, when all these things had been accomplished, each returned home joyfully and from that day onwards they have been free of that kind of plague.

Note: This is the only known reference to a twelfth-century plague in Reading.

MIRACLE V

At the aforementioned time, when the Lord gathered a harvest of his people with the daughters of his quiver and decimated his sons, there was a man of Reading called Edward, surnamed Haver, who was overcome by a sickness and became very seriously ill, mainly with hectic fever. When the man had been suffering from this illness for some considerable time, sickness was added to sickness, pain to pain, and quinsy to fever. And since they came together they were particularly deleterious because they were linked to each other. The fever fed upon the wretched man's wretched limbs and a serious blockage in his throat denied his body food and drink. The poor man could neither bring up nor swallow anything. But now the hardship of the earlier fever seemed light and moderate, compared with that of the quinsy which followed. Now his spirit disdained all food and he drew near to the gates of death. He passed several days in this agony before water of the blessed James was sent to him from the monastery of the monks of Reading and, filled with faith, he drank it down and, against all hope, took it into his body. The tumour in his throat at once went down, the blockage disappeared, and he recovered his voice, which had been all but stifled, and so through the wholesome antidote of the drink he came out in a sweat and after a short while was fully restored to health. He got up healthy and well and - something he had not done for a long time - he ate and drank, and gave worthy and due thanks to God and St. James.

Note: Edward Haver of Reading is otherwise unknown.

MIRACLE VI

Some days later this man's daughter developed the same sickness as her father earlier. The father was anxious for his daughter on this account and was driven to have recourse to the remedy which he had tried previously. He therefore requested and obtained the aforesaid water of the aforesaid apostle and gave it to his daughter to drink. When she had drunk it all, she who had been sick very quickly regained her strength and was restored to health, and coming to the monastery along with her father she made votive offerings to St. James.

[**Miracle VII**] Quedam mulier nomine Goda, uxor cuiusdam militis de Herefordsira qui Herewardus dicebatur, plurimum infirmata et pene desperata, misit Rading' propter aquam beati Iacobi. Que cum allata fuisset fecit se deferri ad ecclesiam ut in domo Domini de Domino confidens sanctificationis liquorem aliquatenus dignius sumere valeret. Quo delata, facta oratione sancti liquaminis suscepit antidotum. Vix vitalia liquor attigerat, vix incaluerat, et iam operatus est salutem in medio eius. Nam dolor effugatur, natura refoscillatur, spiritus roboratur, ita ut sana surgeret et letabunda et laudans nullo adminiculante in propria unde baiulorum manibus paulo ante delata fuerat pedes remearet. Audientes et videntes que gloriose fiebant in ea dederunt laudem Deo.

[**Miracle VIII**] Puella quedam de Esexia nomine Adeliza, cuiusdam clerici filia, in die sancto Parascevense valde diluculo ut oves emulgeret ad ovile perrexit. Cui redeunti apparuit et occurrit quedam phantastica effigies, habens faciem quasi hominis, aspectum et speciem tanquam mortui in funus et sepulturam preparati. Quo viso mulier expavit et contremuit, gelidusque stetit circum precordia sanguis. Phantasma migrans ocius pertransiit. Mulier fugiens et aufugiens, quantocius preterit. Come illi steterunt; pili [fo. 172v] inhorruerunt; confunditur sensus; tollitur intellectus. Tandem domum veniens et ignem aspiciens, in faciem corruit et tanquam in insaniam versa agitari enormiter cepit, omnemque gestum et motum insanienti simillimum pretendit. Sopore tandem superveniente hiis finem fecit. Obdormivit autem sinistro brachio sub mamilla nudis costis superposito. Cum vero evigilaret et in se rediret, predictum brachium aruerat et iam ypocondriis inheserat, ita ut cutis a cute discerni, caro a carne disiungi, non posset, sed et os ossibus incumbens vementem dolorem ingessit. Igitur prefata puella a finibus suis egressa, circuivit terram et perambulavit eam, per sanctorum loca querens remedium et salutis solatium. Sed multo tempore in hac peregrinatione consumpto, cum nichil uspiam profecisset, pertesa miserie et plena amaritudine repatriavit, et inacta desperavit. Post pusillum temporis apparuit beatus Iacobus cuidam matrone illius territorii, 'Domine', dicens ad eam, 'Dic Adelize illi ut eat Rading' ad monasterium sancte Marie, quia ibi sanitatem recipiet.' Hanc visionem cum semel et secundo vidisset et super hoc dissimulanter egisset, tertio qui bis apparuerat apparuit,

MIRACLE VII

A certain woman named Goda, wife of a knight of Herefordshire called Hereward, grievously ill and almost without hope, sent to Reading for water of the blessed James. And when it had been brought, she had herself carried to church so that, in the house of the Lord and trusting in the Lord, she could somewhat more worthily drink the sanctifying liquid. And when she had been taken there, she prayed and received the antidote of the sacred liquid'. Scarcely had the liquid touched and warmed her vitals, when it immediately brought about a cure within her. For the pain was removed, her body was revived and her spirit strengthened so that she got up healed, and, full of joy and praise, without anyone's assistance she returned on foot to her home from which she had shortly before been carried in the arms of bearers. Those who heard and saw these things gloriously performed in her gave praise to God.

Note: Both Goda and her husband have proved unidentifiable.

MIRACLE VIII

A certain girl of Essex named Alice, daughter of a clerk, went to the sheepfold on Good Friday, just as day was breaking, to milk the sheep. On her way back there appeared in front of her a ghastly figure with a face like a man's and the appearance and form as though of a dead man prepared for his funeral and burial. When she saw it the damsel was terrified and began to tremble, and the blood froze round her heart. The phantom very quickly left her and disappeared. The damsel fled and ran away as fast as she could. Her hair stood on end and bristled, her senses were confused and she lost her reason. At length she got home and, catching sight of some fire, she threw it in her face. She became seriously disturbed, as though she had gone mad, and acted and moved very much like a mad woman. Eventually sleep came over her and put an end to these ravings. However, she slept with her left arm resting on her bare ribs below her breast. When she awoke and came to herself, the aforesaid arm had withered and had now become attached to her abdomen, in such a way that skin could not be parted from skin, nor flesh separated from flesh, and also one bone pressing on others caused her violent pain. Therefore, the aforesaid girl left home and went round the land seeking from the shrines of saints a cure and aid to health. But after spending a great deal of time on this pilgrimage and deriving no benefit anywhere, she returned home worn out with grief and full of bitterness and gave up in despair. After a very short while the blessed James appeared to a certain matron of that region. 'Lady,' he said to her, 'Tell Alice to go to Reading, to the monastery of St. Mary, because there she will receive her health.' When she had seen this vision once and a second time and had neglected to do anything about it, he who had appeared twice appeared a

eam de inobedientia increpans, et sub interminatione ultionis iniungens, ut que viderat predicte puelle nuntiaret. Quo facto, prefata puella spem convalescendi concipiens, Rading' profecta est. Ubi cum sex diebus moram fecisset, et nichil profecisset, desperans repatriare die sequenti proposuit. Correpta igitur a sancto apostolo et in sompnis admonita, de uno nummo quem solum habebat ceram comparavit, et candelam sibi preparari fecit. Ad ecclesiam igitur veniens, cum visionem suam sacriste exposuisset, introducta et altari admissa missam audivit et candelam suam optulit. Post missarum solempnia Willelmus supprior Rading' tulit capsam qua manus sancti Iacobi continebatur, et eam tenuit super brachium mulieris quod arverat et costis inheserat, Nicholao monacho aquam desuper effudente, et inde brachium irrigante, ilico virtus apostolica que emortua fuerant revivicare, que ligata dissolvere, que conglutinata cepit disiungere. Illa igitur convalescere incipiente, factus est dolor intensior, anxietas acutior, tortio vehementior. Post duarum autem vel circiter trium horarum spatium, brachium a latere disiunctum in gremium suum decidit, cui in signum et testimonium miraculi cutis a costis avulsa adhuc ex brachio dependebat. Brachium adhuc plurimum fetebat et dolebat, nimisque intumescebat. Aliquandiu autem moram faciens in ecclesia ex toto in perfectam convaluit salutem, nullo pristine infirmitatis inditio, nullo debilitatis vestigio in ea ulterius remanente. Apostolicis igitur obligata beneficiis eius sese mancipavit obsequiis, manutergia ecclesie ceteraque lineia ornamenta abluens, corpori tantum necessaria accipiebat, solicitumque obsequium Deo et apostolo aliquandiu exhibebat donec, a quodam fabro seducta et abducta, sese in eius coniugium resolveret et laudabile conscientie propositum sine remissione concluderet.

[**Miracle IX**] Erat quidam monachus Rading' nomine Thomas de territorio eodem oriundus, qui subitum capitis tumorem incurrens, acutissime cepit urgeri. Crevit igitur tumor et excrevit, tumori tumorem adiciens, dolorem dolore instaurans. Tumor igitur dilatatus in genas descendit et faciem usque quaque occupavit, frons faciei, gene superciliis occurrere, et visum intercludere minabantur. Tandem tumor industria cuiusdam medici ad tempus compescitur, sed

third time, rebuking her sharply for her disobedience and commanding her under threat of punishment to inform the aforesaid girl of what she had seen. This done, the aforesaid girl, building up her hope of recovery set out for Reading. When she had spent six days there and had received no benefit, she lost heart and decided to return home the next day. At this point she was forestalled by the holy apostle and, advised to do so in a dream, she bought wax with the only coin she had and had a candle prepared for herself. Coming then to the church, she related her vision to the sacrist and was led in and admitted to the altar, where she heard mass and offered her candle. After mass, William, sub-prior of Reading, brought the reliquary in which the hand of St. James was kept and held it over the damsel's arm which had withered and become attached to her ribs, while the monk Nicholas poured water over and bathed her arm with it. Immediately the power of the apostle began to revive what had been dead, to loosen what had been bound and to separate what had been joined together. Now, as she began to recover, the pain became more intense, her agony more acute and her torment more grievous. But after about two or three hours, the arm came away from her side and fell into her lap and, as a sign and witness of the miracle, the skin had been torn from her ribs and was still hanging down from her arm. The arm still smelt and ached badly and became very swollen. But after she had spent some considerable time in the church, she completely recovered to perfect health, with no sign of her former infirmity and no trace of her disability remaining any longer on her. Accordingly, being grateful for the favours of the apostle, she devoted herself to his service. She washed the towels and other linen dressings of the church, receiving only the necessaries for her body, and she gave devoted service to God and the apostle for quite a time, until she was seduced and abducted by a certain smith and became his wife, putting an end without leave to the praise-worthy intentions of her conscience.

Note: The dates of William, sub-prior of Reading, are unknown, but an Anselm occurs as sub-prior of Reading in a document dating probably from the 1180s (*Reading Cartularies*, ii. no. 704) and a Simon occurs as sub-prior in a document of 1186 x 1213 (*Ibid*, no. 839).

MIRACLE IX

There was a certain monk of Reading named Thomas, a native of those parts, who suddenly developed a tumour on his head which caused him very acute pain. This tumour grew bigger and bigger, adding tumour to tumour and reinforcing pain with pain. The swollen tumour spread down on to his cheeks and completely filled his face; his forehead joined up with his face and his cheeks came up to his eyebrows threatening to stop his sight. At length the tumour was checked for a time by the efforts of some doctor, but

post aliquantulum temporis redivivus adolevit, et vehementius et intensius succrevit. Tantus erat oculorum pruritus ut supercilia expilaret, palpebras scalpendo contereret, oculos perfoderet, nisi manum violenter reprimeret, et affectum noxium cohiberet[a] Igitur cum non esset qui adiuvaret,[26] clamavit ad Dominum et ad sanctum Iacobum ut eum liberaret. Vocavit igitur Willelmum tunc temporis suppriorem, rogans et obsecrans quatenus capud suum sacra manu beati Iacobi signaret. Aiebat enim se confidere et de meritis apostoli presumere, ut si ei vivere ulterius expediret convalesceret, et tanti patris patrocinio plenam sanitatem reciperet. Factus est igitur postquam signatum est capud infirmi manu apostolica, pannum lineum aqua beati apostoli humectavit, quo capud involuit et undique circumtexit. Nec mora pruritus cepit sedari, dolor mitigari, tumor decrescere, minui et rarescere. Post biduum in perfectam solidatus salutem, cum ceteris monachis ad processionem ivit nulla precedentis morbi preferens inditia, nulla tumoris preteriti pretendens vestigia.

[**Miracle X**]
Cuiusdam monachi Radingensis Iohannis nomine manus aruerat, et sensum motabilem [fo. 173r] magna ex parte amiserat. Manum enim non potuit erigere nec quicquam si apprehenderet retinere. Itaque ad remedium multis expertum accedens, aqua sancti Iacobi manum aridam perfudit et statim in ipsa die motum pristinum et agilitatem optate habitudinis manus accepit,

[**Miracle XI**] Apud Collingeburnam degebat quedam mulier quam dirus dolor viscerum diutina fatigatione decoxerat. Que quadam nocte obdormiens, vidit in visu beatum Iacobum ipsam hortantem ut, si salutem consequi cuperet, Rading' cum candela sua iret. Et adiecit qui sibi apparuerat quia, si illa die quam ei prefixit[b] Rading' veniret, sacram manum beati Iacobi aspiceret et optatam salutem perciperet. Prohibuit etiam ne candelam quam fecerat Saresberiam sicut proposuerat deferret sed Rading'. Facto autem mane visionis non immemor firmavit faciem suam ut iret Rading'. Cum autem Rading' veniret, invenit ibi comitem Gloecestrensem cum uxore sua pluribusque non mediocris [c]potentie proceribus,[c] qui ab abbate optinuerant ut sibi liceret manum sancti Iacobi aspicere et adorare. Igitur hac occasione, sicut ei predictum fuerat, manum sancti Iacobi aspexit et adoravit. Potita vero sacre manus benedictione mulier

a. *Ms* choiberet.
b. *Ms* pret'fixit.
c-c. *Ms* proceribus potentie, *marked for transposition.*

26. Ps.22:11

after a little while it revived and grew again, swelling very much more violently. His eyes itched so much that he would have pulled out his eyebrows, worn away his eyelids with scratching and picked out his eyes, if he had not kept his hand down by force and held the harmful urge in check. In this state, since there was no-one who could help, he called to the Lord and St. James to deliver him. Accordingly he called William, at that time sub-prior, asking and beseeching him to make a sign on his head with the sacred hand of St. James. For he said he believed and trusted in the merits of the apostle, so that, if it was right for him to live longer, he might be healed and receive full health from the good offices of so great a father. And so it turned out that, after the invalid's head had been signed with the apostle's hand, he moistened a linen cloth with water of the blessed apostle and bound up his head with it, covering it all round. At once the itching began to subside, the pain began to ease and the tumour started to go down, growing less and withering away. After two days he was restored to perfect health and went in procession with the rest of the monks, showing no sign of his former sickness nor trace of the tumour which had disappeared.

Note: On William, the sub-prior, see note to miracle VIII.

MIRACLE X

The hand of a certain monk of Reading named John had withered and had for the most part lost its power of movement. He could neither raise his hand nor keep hold of anything he might grasp. Coming therefore to the remedy which had been tried by many people, he bathed his withered hand with water of St. James and immediately, on that very day, his hand acquired its original movement and its habitual agility which he longed for.

MIRACLE XI

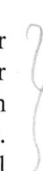

At Collingbourne there lived a certain woman who had been wasting away in long drawn out weariness from a frightful pain in her entrails. When she was asleep one night she saw the blessed James in a dream urging her, if she wished to recover her health, to go to Reading with her candle. And he who had appeared to her added that, if she came to Reading on the day which he appointed for her, she would see the sacred hand of the blessed James and obtain the cure which she desired. He also told her not to take the candle which she had made to Salisbury, as she had planned, but to Reading. In the morning she remembered her dream and set her face to go to Reading. Now, when she got to Reading she found the earl of Gloucester there with his wife and several great and powerful lords, who had obtained from the abbot permission to see and adore the hand of St. James. And so taking this opportunity, as had been foretold to her, she saw and adored the hand of St. James. And having secured the blessing of the sacred hand, the woman

cuius venter amaricatus fuerat sanitatem recepit. Qua percepta quid sibi acciderit qua revelatione advenerit palam omnibus enarravit.

[**Miracle XII**] Quedam mulier de Suffolchia cum filia sua Rading' venit in die sancto Pentecostes. Hanc autem adolescentulam a nativitate sua ita natura dampnaverat ut a genibus et infra nulla ossuum solidatas tibiis inesse videretur, nec flectendi vel extendendi poplitem facultas. Tibie enim carne et cute obducte tanquam cartillagines plicari potuerunt et brachio circumduci. Hanc autem spe salutis recuperande mater circumquaque per sanctorum loca circumduxerat, ut sanctis intervenientibus Dominus ei propiciaretur et eam consolidare et erigere dignaretur. Igitur, cum in processione capsam qua manus beati Iacobi continebatur intuita esset puella, divine virtutis in se sensit suffragium et apostolice presentie adiutorium. Tibie enim eius ilico rigescere et in ossei roboris ceperunt convalescere. Quibus convalescentibus protinus consolidate sunt bases eius et plante, ita ut in brevi in sanitatem fortius firmaretur et ambulandi facultatem nancisceretur.

[**Miracle XIII**] Miraculo huic simillimum in quodam puero de Rading' orto nomine Willelmo contigisse novimus, quem ab ineunte etate diris indignationis sue legibus natura ita multaverat ut, contracto utroque poplite, spasmum pati putaretur. Sed et tanta erat tibiarum gracilitas ut humani pollicis grossiciem nullatenus excedere videretur. In nocte vero Natalis Domini, cum annua devotione populus ad ecclesiam congregatus divina audiret misteria, puer prefatus ad ecclesiam delatus et ante altare quod vulgus sancti Iacobi[a] altare appellare consuevit collocatus, celitus visus est confortari et in illis partibus quas debilitas devinxerat corroborari. Nervi enim qui arefacti et contracti fuerant remitti et humectari, ossa ingrossescere et consolidari ceperunt. Surrexit igitur puer columpne innitens que est a dextris altaris ubi iacuerat. Adhuc enim surgere insolitus et gradi non expertus, se sibi credere non audebat, quia tam de usu quam de potentia diffidebat. Post pusillum primitias ambulandi arripiens, quod difficile est gressui infirmo per gradus ad altare ascendit. Et ut claresceret cuius

a. *Ms* Iacacobi.

whose stomach had been diseased was cured and, after receiving her health, she openly told everyone what had happened to her and how it had come about as the result of a vision.

Note: It is uncertain whether this woman came from Collingbourne Ducis or Collingbourne Kingston, both in Wiltshire. The earl of Gloucester is unidentifiable.

MIRACLE XII

A certain woman of Suffolk came to Reading with her daughter on the holy day of Whitsun. Now, nature had so condemned this girl from birth, that from her knees down she appeared to have no firm bones in her shins and could not bend or straighten her knees. For her shins, were full of flesh and skin and could be folded over like gristle and pulled round with her arm. In the hope of recovering her health, her mother, had taken her around the shrines of saints everywhere, in order that by the intervention of the saints the Lord might have mercy on her and deign to heal and raise her up. So then, when the girl saw in procession the reliquary in which the hand of the blessed James was kept, she felt the aid of divine power for her and the assistance of the apostle's presence. In fact her shins immediately began to harden and gain strength as firm bones, and as they did so her feet and the soles of her feet instantly hardened, with the result that in a short while she was very fully restored to health and acquired the power of walking.

MIRACLE XIII

We have heard that a miracle very similar to this happened to a certain boy called William, a native of Reading; from his birth nature had so punished him by the awful laws of her indignation, that, with both legs shrunken, he was regarded as a spastic. Moreover, his legs were so thin that they appeared no thicker than a human thumb. On Christmas Eve, however, the people had assembled in the church in their annual devotion and were listening to the divine mysteries, when the aforesaid boy was carried to the church and set down in front of the altar which the people have been accustomed to call the altar of St. James. He seemed to be cured from heaven and to receive strength in those limbs which had been seized by lameness. Indeed, the withered and shrunken sinews began to slacken and become moist, and his bones began to grow and harden. As a result, the boy stood upright supporting himself by the pillar standing to the right of the altar where he had lain. Hitherto he had been unaccustomed to standing upright and incapable of walking and so he was afraid to trust himself, because he lacked confidence in his ability and strength. After a little while he mastered the basic principles of walking and climbed up the steps to the altar, a difficult operation for the feet of a disabled person. And in order to show by whose

meritis erectus fuisset, ante imaginem beati Iacobi ibi depictam substitit cornibusque altaris adhesit, tanquam salvatori suo gratias referens vel ei adherere cupiens. Tota illa nocte et die Nativitatis Dominice nulla frigoris ingruentia, nulla famis vel sitis inclementia valuit nec voluit separari. Sequente vespere sanus recessit, et ulterius non sunt infirmata vestigia eius.

[**Miracle XIV**] In Burchildebiria villisque Burchildeb(ir)ie conterminis pestilentia immensa immerserat, que homines et iumenta, oves et boves, insuper et peccora campi tabe mortalitatis infecerat et partem maximam contriverat. Cum vero nimium invalesceret et in suo cursu medium iter haberet, Rogerus abbas Radingensis Burchildeb(ir)iam venit, qui manum beati Iacobi ad regem detulerat et iam secum retulerat. Interventu autem Petri decani Burchildebirie, in veneratione beati Iacobi ibidem missas celebravit, et post missas confecta aqua benedicta capsam qua sacra manus includebatur intinxit. Et elevata manu apostoli, cum in locum quendam excelsum discedens venisset, provinciam[a] dira calamitate laborantem benedixit et aquam benedictam prefatam per domos et familias aspergi communuit. Factumque est ita. Eadem die et hora cessavit mortalitas, pestis evanuit immanitas, tam in [fo. 173v] hominibus quam in iumentis.

[**Miracle XV**] Miraculi huius memoriam prefatus monachus perpetuare satagens, in monte prefate benedictionis crucem unam ligneam erigere proposuit. Que cum cogitasset, didicit quia in nemore cuiusdam militis sibi proximi et amici tale lignum quod ad hoc esset idoneum presectum iacuit, quod miles nullo artium[b] ingenio vel conamine a loco quo ceciderat ammovere poterat, sed ibidem iam per biennium iacuerat.

a. Ms provintiam.
b. Later altered in Ms to artificum.

merits he had been raised up, he stopped in front of the picture of the blessed James painted there and grasped the ends of the altar, as though he were giving thanks to his saviour or trying to embrace him. Throughout that night and Christmas Day he could not and would not be drawn away by any assault of the cold or any pang of hunger or thirst. On Christmas evening he went away healed and there remain no longer any signs of his lameness.

MIRACLE XIV (1158-65)

In Bucklebury and in the villages around Bucklebury there had broken out a great plague which had infected men and beasts, sheep and oxen, and even the flocks in the field, with a deadly disease and had wiped out the greater part of them. But when it was getting a very strong hold and spreading without check, Roger, abbot of Reading, who had taken the hand of the blessed James to the king and had now brought it back with him, came to Bucklebury. And at the request of Peter, dean of Bucklebury, he celebrated mass there in honour of blessed James and, after mass, he blessed some water and dipped in it the reliquary containing the sacred hand. And with the apostle's hand held aloft he went out and came to a particular high spot and blessed the area suffering from the awful disaster, and gave instructions for the aforesaid water which had been blessed to be sprinkled on the homes and households. And this was done. On the same day and at that very hour the plague ceased and the cruel pestilence disappeared both among men and beasts.

Note: Bucklebury was a Berkshire manor belonging to Reading Abbey. This plague is otherwise unknown. The naming of Abbot Roger dates the miracle to 1158 x 65 and identifies the king as Henry II. The reference to Peter, dean of Bucklebury, is interesting. He is clearly the same as the monk who erected the memorial in the following story and, therefore, as a monk, cannot have been a rural dean. In all probability he was the monastic keeper of the abbey's Bucklebury estate and the designation 'dean' was derived no doubt from the Cluniac origins of Reading Abbey. Cf., B. L. Cott. Vesp. E xxv, fo. 159v, fo. 197v; and see my note on 'The Monastic dean of Leominster', *E.H.R.,* lxxxiii (1968).

MIRACLE XV (1158-65)

Intent on preserving the memory of this miracle, the aforesaid monk proposed to erect a wooden cross on the hill where the above blessing had taken place. And when he had given the matter some thought, it came to him that in the wood of a certain knight, who was a neighbour and friend of his, there lay some felled timber just right for his project, which the knight had been unable, by any skill or effort of experts, to move from the spot where it had fallen. In fact, it had lain in the same place for two years.

Monachus itaque lignum predictum sibi donare optinuit. Ligno autem carro imposito, dum boves illud trahere conarentur omnia trahentium instrumenta quasi fila aranee in primo conamine disrupta sunt. Restes denuo restaurati et triplicati secundo et tercio comminuuntur. Quo visu, mirantur singuli, stupescunt universi. Perpendens tandem prefatus monachus quod antiquus hostis signo crucis per quam victus fuerat semper invideat, misit sub festinatione qui aquam beati Iacobi de qua superius mentionem fecimus sibi deferret, ex qua iuga boum, restes, lignum, et carrum bovesque conspersit, et carrum agitari precepit. Ilico cum summa facilitate boves carrum trahentes processerunt, nullumque de cetero impedimentum in hoc opere habuerunt. Nec erat iam opus boves minare vel urgere, qui tanquam celitus incitati ceperunt ad locum destinatum properare. Unde qui aderant admirantes, ut miraculum certius experirentur, substiterunt, hinc et a longe pedetentim subsequentes, rei exitum consideraverunt. Boves itaque per se properantes ad locum destinatum pervenerunt, ibique subsistentes nullo cohibente[a] nullatenus ultra procedure voluerunt. Quo in loco ex ipso ligno crux facta et in memoriam miraculi pretaxati erecta est.

g. *Ms* choibente.

The monk persuaded him to give him the aforesaid timber, but when the timber had been loaded on to a cart and the oxen struggled to pull it, at the first try all the harnesses snapped like a spider's web. The ropes were twice repaired but both the second and third time they broke. When they saw this everyone was struck with amazement. At length the said monk, marking well the fact that the old enemy always hates the sign of the cross by which he was vanquished, sent someone at great speed to fetch him the water of blessed James to which we referred above, and with it he sprinkled the yoke of the oxen, the ropes, timber, cart and oxen, and ordered the cart to be moved. At once, and with the greatest of ease, the oxen were able to move forward pulling the cart and experienced no further hindrance in their task. And now there was no need to threaten or goad the oxen, for, as though driven on by heaven, they hurried away to the appointed place. At this, those who were there hung back in amazement that they were undoubtedly witnessing a miracle and, following slowly a long way behind, they pondered on the way things had turned out. However, the oxen rushed on by themselves and arrived at the appointed place, where they stopped without anyone restraining them and refused to go any further. And at that spot a cross was constructed out of the wood and set up as a memorial of the miracle described above.

Note: This story helps to explain two charters of Jocelin, bishop of Salisbury (1142-84), in one of the Reading Abbey cartularies. In one of these (*Reading Cartularies*, i. no. 692), the bishop grants an indulgence of 40 days to all of his diocese who, on the vigil or feast of St. Mary Magdalen, visit, and make an offering to, the holy place built in honour of God and St. Mary Magdalen at Bucklebury by the cross of St. James. In the other (*Ibid*, no. 693), the bishop grants an indulgence to those who visit the chapel of St. Mary Magdalen near *(iuxta)* Bucklebury and its graveyard, which he has dedicated. The cross of the first of these charters is obviously the one referred to in Miracle XV. There are good reasons for supposing that the chapel was in the manor of Marlston, held in the later twelfth century by Geoffrey Martel, for it is clear that the chapel on his manor was then in the parish of Bucklebury. (B. L. Add. Ch. 19610). It is not clear whether the chapel was built as a consequence of the quelling of the plague described in No. XIV, but, if that were the case, the dedication to St. Mary Magdalen might indicate that the plague had been one of leprosy, since her name was frequently associated with the disease and its cure. Cf. the foundation of a leper hospital dedicated to her in Reading Abbey by Abbot Anscher, 1130 x 35 (*Reading Cartularies*, i. no. 221).

[**Miracle XVI**] Paucis postea evolutis diebus, quidam de Bradefeld nervorum contractione incurvus, nocturna visione admonitus, ad locum quo crux erecta fuit sese deferre fecit. Quo aliquandiu orationi deditus, sui corporis adeptus est sanitatem et pristinam habilitatem.

[**Miracle XVII**] In villa que Cuserige dicitur quedam matrona nomine Ysembela, uxor Sewali illius ville domini, egritudine miserabili correpta fuit. Interiora sua ita sibi congelari videbantur, ut egritudine instante nullatenus possent calefieri. Vix enim aliquam interpolatum agens diem fremebat et tremebat, tanquam nimio febrium rigore agitata, et quid ipsa ageret vel circa eam ageretur, penitus ignoravit. Tanquam epilentica semianimis in terram cadebat vultumque femine iamiam expirature preferebat. Medicos igitur quamplurimos crebro consuluit, sed a nullo curari potuit.Tandem ad se rediens et mirabilium que per beatum Iacobum fieri audierat recolens, votum vovit Deo et beato Iacobo. Venitque Rading' votum solutura et pro salute sua supplicatura. In ecclesia igitur vigilias votivas excoluens, plenam meruit recipere sospitatem pristinique virtutis antequam discederet integritatem.

[**Miracle XVIII**] Erat in aquilonalibus Anglie partibus cuiusdam divitis bernerius nomine Gilebertus, qui venatus vanitate sat et supra delectatus, non iudicavit inter diem et diem, sed vanitati et voluptati licitum omnem reputans diem, in die sancti Iacobi venandi gratia in silvam properavit, solempnitati non deferens nec apostolo debitam reverentiam exhibens. Cervum igitur quendam[a] cum leporariis insequens diuque insequendo insistens, tandem eum comprehendit. Cum enim congratulari cepisset captioni, supervenit in eum ultio Domini. Videbatur enim ei quasi salsugo sudoris oculis influeret, visumque penitus obduceret. Quem cum extergere niteretur, abstersit et visum. Ad equitaturam suam vix tandem palpando perveniens

a. Interlined in Ms.

MIRACLE XVI (1158-65)

A few days later a man of Bradfield, bent up with shrinking of the sinews, was advised in a dream and had himself brought to the place where the cross had been set up. There he prayed for some time and gained the health and former fitness of his body.

Note: Bradfield is near Bucklebury, Berkshire.

MIRACLE XVII (? before 1147)

In the village of Curridge a certain matron called Ysembela, wife of Sewal, the lord of the village, was overcome by a wretched illness. Her inside seemed so frozen that in the severity of her illness it was impossible to make it warm. In fact, with hardly a day's respite she growled and quaked, as though tormented beyond endurance by the severity of her fever, and was utterly at a loss to know what to do herself or what could be done for her. Like an epileptic she would fall half-dead to the ground and her face was that of a woman already about to breathe her last. She therefore consulted many physicians on several occasions, but failed to be cured by any of them. At length she returned home and, calling to mind the miracles which she had heard had been worked by blessed James, made a vow to God and blessed James. And she came to Reading to fulfil her vow and pray for her health. In the church she diligently observed the vigils she had promised and deservedly underwent a complete cure and, before she went away, recovered her original good health.

Note: Curridge is near Newbury (Berkshire). A certain Sewal held one hide of the King in Curridge and granted it to Waverley Abbey before 1147 *(Victoria County History, Berkshire,* iv. 60). The account of this miracle reads as though Sewal is still in possession of Curridge, but there is no conclusive evidence that the miracle dates from before 1147.

MIRACLE XVIII (1163-87)

In the north of England there was a certain rich man's keeper of hounds named Gilbert, who was over-fond of the vanity of the chase and, drawing no distinction between one day and another, believed that vanity and pleasure were permitted on any day. On St. James' day he cantered into the wood to hunt, paying no regard to the feast and failing to show due reverence to the apostle. And with his hounds he pursued a stag and, keeping on its heels for a good while, he eventually caught it. But when he proceeded to congratulate himself on his prize, the vengeance of the Lord came upon him, for salty perspiration seemed to run into his eyes and entirely cut off his vision. When he tried to wipe it away, he wiped away his sight as well. At length he just managed to grope his way to his horse and

ascendit, et se non sibi sed caballi sui sagacitati committens redire temptavit. Tandem cum labore et dolore reversus, cum aliquandiu permansisset cecus, et nullis colliriis nullisque potuisset curationibus mederi, cepit fieri onerosus quibus fuerat prius gratiosus. Raros enim amicos repperit adversitas, paucissimos paupertas, fere nullos medicantium cecitas, iuxta illud: 'Cum fueris felix multos numerabis amicos. Tempora cum fuerint nebula solus eris'.[27] Seditque in tenebris et in umbra mortis, vinctus mendicitate et morbo. Vix sola coniux sibi remanserat, que ei ducatum prebuit et circumcirca per loca sanctorum deduxit, sed frustra, qui nusquam illuminari potuit. Post multum vero temporis, placuit Domino finem facere eius infirmitati et remedium prestare cecitati. Apparuit igitur ei in visione beatus Iacobus, precipiens ei ut Rading' iret, si lumen oculorum[a] recipere cuperet. Mane surrexit homo et, ducente coniuge, in spe visionis Rading' properavit. Quo proveniens, cum ibidem aliquandiu moraretur et nichil melioraretur, mora impaciens et a spe decidens cecus repatriare disposuit. [fol. 174r] A Rading' discessit et usque ad Bannebiriam pervenit, ubi iterum in sompnis increpatus et admonitus est ut Rading' rediret et in festo sancti apostoli quod instabat, facta sibi candela, promissam sibi salutem expectaret. Radingias denuo reducitur, et in vigilia beati Iacobi cum candela sua in monasterium introducitur. Sequenti die dominus Gilebertus episcopus Londoniensis, pulpitum ascendens et manum sanctissimi apostoli de capsa veteri in novam transferens, populum ex ea benedixit. Quam cum elevaret et benedictionem proferret, oculi prefati ceci ceperunt vehementissime prurire et scintillare. Sanguinee autem gutte, ex concavitatibus oculorum defluentes, genas irrigabant. Ipsa vero hora, ipsoque momento, aperti sunt oculi eius. Erigens itaque capud vultumque ad candelam suam convertens, vidit eam consumptam usque ad plicam condilatam et iamiam ipsam consumpturam. Candelam festinanter sustulit, et lichinum subrigens in laudes beatissimi Iacobi erupit, et sese lumen recepisse propalavit. Sanguinee lacrime, quas oculi produxerant adhuc ex genis hominis qui visum receperat, in testimonium rei geste dependebant. Gaudens igitur pro amore et honore apostoli in Rading' pluribus annis servivit xenodochio quousque, artiore voto tactus intrinsecus, Ierosolimam ivit et laudabile devotionis exordium fine famosiore concludit.

a. Ms occulorum

27. Cf. Prov. 19:4.

mounted, and, putting trust not in himself but in the intelligence of his steed, he attempted the journey home. Eventually, with difficulty and in pain, he got back, but for a long time he remained blind and, unable to be cured by ointments or remedies, he began to become a burden to those among whom he had previously been very popular. In his adversity he found few friends, in his poverty very few, and in his blindness scarcely any physicians, as in the saying, 'When you are successful you will number many friends; in bad times you will be alone'. Bound by poverty and grief he sat in darkness and in the shadow of death. Barely his wife alone had stayed with him to guide him and she took him everywhere round the shrines of saints, but in vain, for nowhere could he regain his sight. But after a long time it pleased the Lord to put an end to his affliction and provide a cure for his blindness. And so blessed James appeared to him in a dream and ordered him to go to Reading if he wished to receive the light of his eyes. In the morning the man arose and with his wife's guidance hastened to Reading in the hope which the dream had given him. Having arrived there he stayed for some considerable time, but experienced no improvement and, impatient at the wait and losing hope, he decided to go home blind. He therefore left Reading and got as far as Banbury, where, again in a dream, he was rebuked and urged to return to Reading, make himself a candle and await the promised cure on the approaching feast of the holy apostle. He was brought back again to Reading and with his candle was led into the monastery on the eve of blessed James. The following day the lord Gilbert, bishop of London, went up on to the screen and, as he transferred the hand of the most holy apostle from the old reliquary to a new one, he blessed the people with it. And when he lifted it up and gave the blessing, the aforesaid man's eyes began to smart keenly and to gleam. Moreover, tears of blood flowed from his eye-sockets and streamed down his cheeks. At that hour, in fact, and at that very moment his eyes were opened. He raised his head and, turning to look at his candle, saw that it had burned down as far as the knotted fold[28] and would go out at any moment. He quickly picked up the candle and, as he pulled up the wick, broke out in praise of most blessed James and announced that he had received his sight. The tears of blood which his eyes had shed were still sticking on the cheeks of the man who had received his sight, in witness of what had happened. Rejoicing then in the love and honour of the apostle, he served many years in the guesthouse at Reading, until, inspired inwardly by a stricter vow, he went to Jerusalem and rounded off his devotion laudably begun by a more renowned conclusion.

Note: Gilbert, bishop of London, is without doubt Gilbert Foliot (1163-87) and not Gilbert the Universal (1128-34). The reference to his having translated the Hand into a new reliquary is of great interest and it is unfortunate that one cannot date this act within limits narrower than those of his episcopate. It seems

28. I.e., the bulge at the base of the candle.

[**Miracle XIX**] Fuit vir vite venerabilis nomine Osbertus, abbas de Nuthleia, honestate celebris, religione laudabilis, qui gravissima oculorum[i] egritudine preventus languere cepit. Colliriis usus, medicaminaque plurima expertus, non solum nichil remedii, verum plurimum aggravationis et dispendii visus est incurrisse. Dolor intensior, cruciatus sentiebatur acutior. Nam si forte solis radium vel alicuius luminis intueretur aspectum, protinus capud transfigi et oculorum orbes sibi videbantur tenebrari. Noctes insompnes, dies duxit pervigiles. Post aliquantum temporis in hoc dolore transacti cum temporibus suis non inveniret requiem nec oculis suis dormitationem, commonitione cuiusdam canonici sui, vovit sese Rading' iturum sanctumque Iacobum peregrinationis[j] sue muneribus veneraturum. Quo voto labiis expresso, ilico angustia sedari, dolor cepit mitigari, ita ut infra triduum missas cantaret et consequenter sanus et incolumis sicut voverat Rading' veniret. Optulit autem beato apostolo procerum cereum pro voti solutione, lumen pro lumine, laudes pro tam celeri exauditione.

[**Miracle XX**] Estonie que Seford' est contigua degebat quedam puella, nomine Ysembela, Iohannis piscatoris filia, que, cum estivo tempore sub divo dormiret, corporis sui habilitatem et agilitatem amisit. Pars enim sinistra a planta pedis usque ad scapulam arverat et vitalem motum perdiderat. Obstupebat manus contracta et immobiliter dependebat a latere tergo vicina. Pes circumflexus pedis officium diffitens, ita pervertebatur ut calcis crates cratis articuli articulorum locum clavellata usurparent.

i *Ms* occulorum
j *Ms* peregnationis

to show a certain bond between the bishop and Reading Abbey and it is worth noting in this respect that Abbot William of Reading was one of those who sent to the pope testimonials for Foliot in 1169 when the latter feared serious action against him by Thomas Becket and the pope *(Becket Materials*, vi. 628-30).

MIRACLE XIX (before 1189)

There was a man of a venerable way of life named Osbert, abbot of Notley, famous for his integrity and laudable in religion, who began to languish in the grip of a most grievous affliction of the eyes. Having tried ointments and several medicines, he not only received no cure, but seemed rather to have grown very much worse and incurred great expense. He suffered more intense pain and more acute torment. If, for example, he happened to look at a ray of the sun or of any lamp, it seemed as if his head was suddenly being pierced and his eyeballs darkened. He spent sleepless nights and ever wakeful days. When he had been for some time in this pain and could find no rest for his head nor sleep for his eyes, on the advice of one of his canons, he vowed to go to Reading and honour St. James with the service of his pilgrimage. And no sooner had he uttered this vow with his mouth than his anguish started to ease and the pain began to go down, so that within three days he was able to sing mass, and so came to Reading as he had vowed fit and well. He presented a tall candle to the blessed apostle in fulfilment of his vow, light for light and praise for so speedy a dispensation.

Note: Osbert was the first abbot of Notley and ruled for 28 years, i.e., 1162 - *c.* 1190 (*Heads of Religious Houses: England and Wales, i, 940-1216,* ed. D. Knowles and others, (2nd edn, Cambridge, 2001), 283-4). Notley Abbey held the church of Caversham, near Reading, and deputed one of its canons to serve it as parish priest (D. Knowles and R. Neville Hadcock, *Medieval Religious Houses, England and Wales, (*London, 1953), 133).

MIRACLE XX (after Feb., 1173)

At *Estonie*, near *Seford*', there lived a girl named Ysembela, daughter of John the fisherman. By sleeping out in the open one summer time she disabled her body and lost her agility. In fact, her left side from the sole of her foot to her shoulder had withered and lost all living movement. Her hand was shrunken and paralysed and hung motionless from her side close to her back. Her foot was bent round and, incapable of acting as a foot, was so twisted that (? her main foot bones took the place of her heel, her toes were in the place of the bones, and the nails of her shoe were where her toes

Itaque puella sibi facta inutilis aliisque miserabilis, a noverca sua plurimis laccessita[a] iniuriis, variis affecta obprobriis. Tandem spem pietatis mentita a noverca commonetur, vel potius compellitur, ut per sanctorum loca salutem suam quereret, si quopiam forte invenire valeret. Verum ipsa sui sollicita et sospitatis cupida cum multa sanctorum loca peragrasset, nichilque profecisset, Cantuariam revertitur ut unde prius inacta discesserat illuc rediens gratiam optineret. Quo cum pervenisset, fatigata labore et depasta dolore, obdormivit. Vidit itaque sanctum Iacobum in visu ad se venientem et multitudinem sanctorum in albis ipsum sequentem. Qui dixit ei, 'Quid hic moraris? Quid hic queris?' Cui illa, 'Salutem meam quero, et sanctum Thomam expecto.' Apostolus respondit, 'Nequaquam hic salutem accipies, sed vade Rading' ad monasterium meum, et ibi convalesces.' At illa, 'Rading' non vidi, et monasterium tuum nescio. Et quomodo possum illuc ire cum sim debilis et infirma, vie nescia et egena? Certe non ibo, nec me incassum ultra fatigabo.' Iterum et iterum instituit apostolus, admonendo ut Rading' iret, profecto asserens quod ibi et non alibi convalesceret. At illa admonenti contraria, promittenti incredula, visa est sibi cum apostolo litigare, et sese Rading' non ituram affirmare Visionem istam cum sepius vidisset et quod admonita fuerat facere neglexisset, nequaquam Cantuarie convalescere potuit, sed post aliquantum tempus spe omni destituta repatriavit. Quam cum noverca sua vidisset, odio iniquo et indignatione replete, ait. 'Heus tu,' inquit, 'Contracta abisti et ecce contracta redisti. Recede', inquit, 'a me et repe quocunque volueris, quia sub tecto meo nequaquam manebis.' [fo. 174v] Itaque opbrobrii satiata, duplicique dolore sauciata, ad domus cuiusdam amite sue divertit. Ubi suscepta, cum amite sue que audierat, que viderat, que perpessa fuerat enarrasset, impegit novissime in visionem quam de sancto Iacobo viderat. Hiis auditis, amita sua, 'Eia!', inquit, 'Pro posse propera, Radingiam ire festina! Nummum quem solum habeo accipe, et ex eo cum Rading' veneris candelam tibi eme.' Igitur puella a finibus illis egressa et versus Rading' progressa, septimana septima illuc pervenit. Introiens igitur ecclesiam, cum candelam suam accendisset, factus est super eam manus Domini, et anxiatus est in ea spiritus eius. Itaque in salutem suam conturbata super pavimentum corruit, et in vocem clamoremque acutissimum prorumpens usquequaque ingemuit. Crines sparsit, capud contudit, corpusque suum ita absque sui respectu ad petram elisit,

a. *Ms* lascessita.

should have been).[29] And the girl, being thus made useless to herself and pitiable to others, was harrassed by her stepmother with many insults and taunted with abuse of various kinds. At length, inventing a hope of mercy, she was advised, or rather compelled, by her stepmother to see whether she could find a cure anywhere at the shrines of saints. But when, distressed at her own plight and eager for a cure, she had gone round many saints' shrines and derived no benefit, she returned to Canterbury hoping that by going back to the place which she had earlier been provoked into leaving she might obtain grace. She was worn out with effort and eaten up with pain when she got there and fell asleep. And in a dream she saw coming towards her St. James followed by a throng of saints in albs. He said to her, 'What are you waiting here for? What do you seek here?' 'I am in search of a cure,' she replied, 'and I am waiting for St. Thomas.' The apostle answered, 'You will certainly not receive a cure here, but go to Reading, to my monastery, and there you will be healed. 'But' she said, 'I have not seen Reading, nor do I know your monastery. And how can I go there when I am crippled and weak, ignorant of the way and penniless? No, I shall not go nor will I tire myself out anymore to no purpose.' The apostle insisted again and again, urging her to go to Reading and declaring without doubt that she would be healed there and nowhere else. But she rejected his advice and refused to believe his promises, seeing fit to argue with the apostle and to maintain that she would not go to Reading. Since she saw this vision many times and omitted to do what she was told, she certainly could not be cured at Canterbury, but after some time she went home completely destitute of all hope. And when her stepmother saw her, she was filled with spiteful hate and indignation, and said, 'Aha, you went away a cripple and, look, you have come back a cripple. Go away from me,' she said, 'and crawl where you will, for you shall certainly not, stay under my roof.' Full of shame, then and wracked by a double pain, she turned aside to the home of one of her aunts. She was taken in there and, when she had told her aunt what she had heard, seen and endured, she came finally to the vision she had seen of St. James. When she heard this, her aunt exclaimed, 'Quick! Hurry as fast as you can and make haste to Reading. Take the only coin I have and when you get to Reading buy yourself a candle with it.' And so the girl left those parts on her journey to Reading and arrived there seven weeks later. She entered the church and, when she had lit her candle, the hand of the Lord came upon her and her spirit was troubled within her. And so it was that, stirred up for her cure, she threw herself on the pavement and, letting out the most piercing cries, screamed in all directions. She shook her hair about, banged her head and dashed her body against the stone with so little consideration

29. The bracketed passage is a suggested translation of an extremely awkward and probably corrupt passage in the original.

ut putari posset se ipsam velle conterere, et qui supererat spiritum extinguere. Post tres fere horas placuit Domino sanare contritiones eius et finem facere infirmitati eius. Reddita sunt igitur que sunt corporis corpori, que sensus sensibilitati. Motu sensibili sensuque percepto motabi, membra que emortua fuerant in usum nature rediviva redierunt, que divaricata ordinem pristinum et officium receperunt. Itaque puella sui compos effecta et sanitatem optatam adepta, a loco quo ceciderat ammovetur et ad altare sancte Marie Magdalene adducitur. Ubi cum se recollocasset, post agonis sui laborem lassa obdormivit. Evigilans autem ad miraculi attestationem et ad inchoate salutis pefectionem, virus sanguineum excreavit. Post excreationem multum sanguinis evomuit. Vomuit et revomuit, donec humor qui nocuerat et qui nocere poterat in posterum ad purum excludi videretur, et sic ipsa sana et hilaris efficeretur. Igitur in perfectam sanitatem corroborata abiit in patriam suam, sanctum Iacobum in Domino, et Dominus in beato Iacobo glorificans.

[**Miracle XXI**] Aquilina filia Reginaldi de Curteneia, desponsata Gileberto Basseth, concepit. Que tempus pregnantium prosequens, venit ad partum, sed non erat virtus pariendi. Igitur preacuta parturientium angustia aliquot diebus cruciata, cum ascitis medicis medicinisque adhibitis nichil proficeret, nullumque lenimen susciperet, nuntiatum est hoc regi Anglorum Henrico, tunc temporis in illis partibus commoranti. Cui rex gemmas lapidesque preciosos quotquot habuit qui parturientibus conferre credebantur transmisit. Sed illis frustra adhibitis et exhibitis diebus et horis momentisque singulis tanto facta est angustia intensior quanto cruciatus diuturnior. Unde cum quatuor diebus totidemque noctibus parturisset nec peperisset, sola mors superesse, finisque instans accelerari credebatur. Maxime autem quia fetus in utere mortuus ex transverso ventris versatus matris alvum sibi hereditaverat in sepulcrum, cuius altera manus per nascendi exitum iam per biduum irretractabiliter dependebat. Iam enim sepultum videbatur mortuum in moriente corpus in corpore, funus in funere, genitum in genitrice. Veruntamen licet destitute, quamvis ab obstetricibus esset desperata, aqua sancti Iacobi de Rading’ allata et illi propinata, principium mortis preripuit, et parturientis cruciatum absolvit.

for herself that one might have thought that she wished to destroy herself and extinguish what life was left in her. After about three hours it pleased the Lord to remedy her distress and put an end to her sickness. And so what she lacked in body and mind were restored to her. And when her lifeless limbs felt the motion of the senses and the sense of movement, they became alive again and recovered their natural fitness, and from a sprawling position resumed their proper place and function. When the girl had thus been made well and received the cure she had longed for, she was moved away from the place where she had fallen and taken to the altar of St. Mary Magdalen. There she laid herself down and, tired out after the agony of her struggle, fell asleep. Then she awoke and coughed up a bloody poison, in witness of the miracle and to round off the incomplete cure. After coughing she vomited up a great deal of blood. Again and again she vomited until the fluid which had harmed her, and could harm her again, seemed to be thoroughly cleared out, and thus she was made well and joyful. Accordingly she left for home completely cured, glorifying St. James in the Lord and the Lord in blessed James.

Note: Estonie has not been identified. *Seford'* might be Seaford in Sussex, but the statement in this story that the girl returned to Canterbury, from which place she had earlier set out, suggests a place in Kent. The reference to St. Thomas of Canterbury dates the miracle after February 1173 when he was canonized.

MIRACLE XXI (1154-89)

Aquilina, daughter of Reginald de Courtenay and wife of Gilbert Basset, conceived and, after the normal period of pregnancy, came to the point of birth, but had not the strength to give birth. She was tormented by extreme agony of labour for some days and received no help or alleviation from the doctors she called nor from the medicines she tried. This was reported to Henry, king of the English, at that time staying in those parts, and the king sent her as many gems and precious stones as he had which were believed to help those in labour. But these were applied and displayed in vain and every day, hour and minute, the longer she suffered, the more intense did the agony become. Therefore, when she had been in labour for four days and as many nights and had not given birth, only death seemed to remain and her end was thought to be rapidly approaching, chiefly because the fetus, being dead in her womb, had turned across her belly and made the mother's womb its own tomb, while one of its hands which had come out in birth continued to hang down for two days and could not be drawn back. In fact, it really looked like a dead body buried in a dying body, a corpse within a corpse, a child within its mother. Nevertheless, although she had lost hope and had no faith in midwives, water of St. James was brought to her from Reading and given to her to drink. This forestalled the onset of death and eased the agony

Nam torture angustia ilico sedatur et anxietate sopor suavissimus illabitur. Quo depressa dormiens et nesciens nullamque penam sentiens partum effudit, et apostolica virtute a mortis faucibus evasit. A sompno tandem salutifero evigilans et sese a sancto Iacobo liberatam comperiens, ipsum apud Rading' sese visitaturam gratiasque relaturam promisit. Moras vero non passa procerum cereum fieri fecit, quem liberatori suo transmisit. Ipsa autem post dies purificationis sue subsecuta votum quod voverat solvit, et pro vita sibi reddita de capite suo quatuor denarios annuatim sese soluturam spopondit.

[**Miracle XXII**] Iohanne filio regis in Hiberniam proficiscente, cuidam de adolescentibus cum eo proficiscentibus, nescio quo casu, confractum est brachium. Qui cum longo tempore nec medicis nec emplastris convalesceret, vovit Rading' iturum, votumque ibi se sancto Iacobo soluturum si meritis eius convalesceret et sanitatem recuperaret. Nec mora redintegratum est brachium et consolidatum. Succedente vero tempore prefatus adolescens[a] venit in Angliam, sed vota que distinxerunt labia sua sancto Iacobo solvere differens, paulo post per consimilis fortunii eventum multatus est. Fracto iterum altero brachio eius in se reversus[b] cepit cogitare que perpessus fuerat, que voverat quod vota non solverat. Compunctus igitur transgressionis sue culpam agnovit, penitensque bachium cereum cum manu fieri fecit, Rading'que ve[fo. 175r]nire festinavit. Voto igitur soluto brachium quod confractum fuerat redintegrationem, quod conquassatum, perfectam recepit consolidationem. Hoc autem exemplo perpendi potest quantum fidei valeat devotio et quantum voti noceat dissimulatio.

a. *Ms* adholescens.
b. *Ms* rereversus.

of her labour, for immediately the sweetest sleep settled on her agonising torment and flowed over her anguish. And as she slept under its influence, unknowingly and feeling no pain, she gave birth and by the apostle's power escaped the jaws of death. Waking at length from this health giving sleep and discovering that she had been delivered by St. James, she promised to visit and thank him at Reading. In fact, brooking no delay, she had a tall candle made and sent it to her deliverer. She herself followed, after the days of her purification, and performed the vow she had sworn, and in return for life which had been restored to her, she promised to pay annually four pence from her chief manor.

Note: Aquilina was the daughter of the Reginald de Courtenay of, *inter alia,* Sutton Courtenay (Berks), who died in 1194 *(Complete Peerage,* iii. 465; iv. 317). As Egelina, she witnessed a charter by her husband, Gilbert Basset, to Bicester Priory in 1182 x 85 *(Monasticon Anglicanum,* vi. 434). In the later twelfth century Gilbert Basset held the manor of Ardington (Berks) and at the end of the century granted to Reading Abbey a perpetual lease of the demesne meadow of that manor (*Reading Cartularies*, ii. no. 662).

MIRACLE XXII (1185)

As the king's son, John, was setting out for Ireland, one of the young men going with him broke his arm, I know not how. And when after a long time it failed to heal in response to physicians and plasters, he vowed to go to Reading and there fulfil his vow to St. James, if he might be healed by his merits and recover his health. And his arm was immediately healed and became sound. In due course this young man came to England, but he neglected to perform to St. James the vows which he had pronounced with his own lips and was shortly afterwards punished by an event of similar misfortune. This time his other arm was broken and he began inwardly to reflect on what he had suffered and the vows which he had made and not fulfilled. Remorsefully, therefore, he admitted the fault of his transgression, penitently had a wax arm with a hand made, and hurried to Reading. And so, when he had fulfilled his vow, his broken and fractured arm was healed and made completely sound. From this case one can see how much it pays to keep one's word and how dangerous it is to dissemble a vow.

Note: The occasion of the first accident was the expedition of Henry II's youngest son, John, newly created Lord of Ireland, which set out from Milford Haven in 1185 *(Gesta Henrici Secundi,* ed. W. Stubbs (Rolls Series), i. 336).

[**Miracle XXIII**] Erat in territorio de Oxonef(ordia) quedam mulier que per biennium curva et contracta lecto decubuit. Adminata est igitur in sompno ut Rading' ad sanctum Iacobum se deferri faceret. A fratre suo igitur bige imposita versus Rading' tetendit. Et factum est dum iret, sanata est. Ubi igitur reddita pedes et absque vehiculo venit cum fratre suo Rading', votivaque oblatione soluta, quid sibi accidisset et quomodo convaluisset cum fratre suo nobis enarravit.

[**Miracle XXIV**] Quidam miles nomine Robertus de Stanfordia febre acerrime corripitur, et aliquandiu affligitur. Venit igitur Rading' pro salute sua oraturus et beatum apostolum deprecaturus. Post orationem autem rogavit de aqua beati Iacobi sibi aliquantisper propinari. Quam cum gustasset, ilico operata est salutem in medio eius. Cepit autem vomere et revomere, donec noxius humor evacuaretur et febrilis calor ad purum per vomitum purgaretur. Letabundus igitur et laudans ad propria sanus remeavit.

[**Miracle XXIVa**] Similimodo similique medicina a consimili infirmitate sanatus est alius miles nomine Radulfus Gibuinus sed et tot alii tam viri quam femine ut eorum numerum stilo nequeam comprehendere.

[**Miracle XXV**] Comes Bulonie Mattheus, frater Philippi comitis Flandrensis, cum Henrico tercio rege Anglorum cum Drincurtam obsedisset, in die sancti Iacobi regi importunus erat ut castellum invaderet et expugnare temptaret. Rex autem et optimates illius honorem beato apostolo deferentes, nullatenus illo die asserverunt sese audere arma movere. Comes autem prefatus efferus et super hiis indignans postulavit ut predam et spolia quecunque illo die adquireret sibi retinere liceret. Quo impetrato, multis milibus pugnatorum sibi sociatis castellum prefatum obpugnare aggressus est. In primo igitur conamine

MIRACLE XXIII

There was a certain woman in the Oxford region who had been confined to bed for two years, bent up and shrunken. And she was advised in a dream to have herself taken to St. James at Reading. Her brother, therefore, set her in a two-wheeled carriage and she set out for Reading. And it happened that as she went she was cured. And from the place where she was healed she came with her brother to Reading on foot, without the vehicle, and, when she had made her votive offering, she and her brother told us what had happened to her and how she had been cured.

MIRACLE XXIV

A certain knight named Robert of Stanford was overtaken and long afflicted by a very severe fever. He therefore came to Reading to pray for a cure and plead with the blessed apostle. And after prayer he asked that water of blessed James be given to him to drink for a little while. No sooner had he tasted it than it brought about a cure within him. He proceeded to vomit again and again until the harmful fluid was brought up and the feverish heat was reduced by the vomiting. Full of joy and praise he returned home cured.

Note: Robert of Stanford has proved unidentifiable.

MIRACLE XXIVa[30]

In a similar way and by a similar remedy another knight named Ralph Gibuin was cured of a similar disease, as also were so many others, both men and women, that I cannot cover them all in this account.

Note: ·A Ralph Gibewin is found in possession of lands in Liscombe, Soulbury and Wavendon (Bucks) in Richard I's reign. (*Pipe Rolls 3 and 4 Richard I*, 109,111, 201, 203).

MIRACLE XXV (1173)

Matthew, count of Boulogne, brother of Philip, count of Flanders, had laid siege to Driencourt with Henry III, King of the English, and on St. James' day bullied the king to enter the castle and attempt to take it by storm. But the king and his magnates, showing honour to the blessed apostle, declared that they would in no way dare to take up arms that day. The aforesaid count was furious and indignant with them and demanded that he should be allowed to keep whatever booty and spoils he might take that day. When this was agreed many thousands of warriors joined with him and he advanced to storm the aforesaid castle. At the first attempt, however,

30. The MS does not make this a separate miracle.

sagittula quedam quam vulgus ‘pilam’ vocat, tanquam celitus missa, sub patella genu eius infigitur. Quo vulnerato, exercitus circumquaque cepit declinare et ab oppugnatione desistere. Ipse vero ad hospitium delatus, et per momenta singula acrius et acrius cruciatus, tandem a demonio arripitur et aliquandiu affligitur, et sic indignam presumptionis sue audaciam mors digna punivit.

[**Miracle XXVI**] Quidam fratrum de domo venerabili canonicorum Mertonie gravi infirmitate preventus, nomine Rogerus cognomento Hosatus, languere cepit. Erat autem langor[a] fortissimus, ut vix in eo pre dolore remaneret alitus. Venter et vitalia vehementi dolore et tumore distenta dolebant, sed et totum corpus circumquaque tanti tamque intensi morbi acumine gravatum fuerat ut nichil de eo nisi sors ultima resolutionis speraretur. Dum igitur dolor diutinus aliquandiu occupasset, omnia et morbus, mortis preambulus, in suo cursu medium iter haberet, salus ei a regalibus sedibus venit. Divertebant enim hospitandi gratia duo fratres de Rading’ manum beati Iacobi deferentes, quam rex Henricus secundus transfretaturus ad se deferri fecerat, ut eam votiva devotione prosequeretur et apostolice manus tutamine et benedictione mare ingressurus comuniretur. Prefatus igitur Rogerus, qui prius desperans et desperatus penitus videbatur, in tanti hospitis adventu spe potissima potitus, quod corpore non valuit corde gestivit, quod pedibus non potuit affectibus apostolicis reliquiis occurrit, opus fidei consecuturus, spei premia percepturus.

a. *Sic in Ms.*

a type of small arrow, commonly called a pila,[31] shot as it were from heaven, lodged under his knee-cap. At this injury the army began to fall back on all sides and abandon the assault. And he himself was carried back to his tent, in more and more acute pain as each moment passed, and was eventually seized by an evil spirit which tormented him for a considerable time. And in this way a fitting death punished the shameful audacity of his arrogance.

Note: This story is not directly related to the Hand of St. James or to Reading. The incident described took place during the serious rebellion against Henry II in 1173, the king mentioned here being the eldest son of Henry II, who was crowned king in his father's lifetime in 1170 and is frequently named in unofficial records of the later twelfth century as Henry III. He never became sole king, in fact, for he predeceased his father in 1183. Ralph de Diceto gives another account of the death of Matthew, count of Boulogne, which, oddly enough, mentions the Hand of St. James. According to him the count was mortally wounded on the feast of St. James (25 July), 1173, as an act of divine vengeance, chiefly because on the same feast five years earlier he had solemnly sworn fealty to Henry II in the presence of, and having touched, holy relics which included the Hand of St. James, and was now in rebellion against him. Ralph de Diceto says that the wounding took place during an assault on the castle of Arches, immediately following the capitulation of the castle of Driencourt *(Opera Historica,* ed. W. Stubbs, (Rolls Series) I, 373).

MIRACLE XXVI (1154-89)

A certain brother of the venerable house of canons at Merton, named Roger Hosatus, was stricken by a serious illness and began to grow weak. Indeed so extreme was his weakness that there was hardly any life left in him, only pain. His belly and vital parts ached with severe pain from a swollen tumour, but in addition his entire body was so affected in every part by the piercing agony of this fierce and intense disorder that there was no hope for him but the ultimate fate of death. However, when the long drawn out pain had engulfed him for a considerable time and his sickness, the forerunner of death, was not checked, a cure came to him from the king's throne. For there turned aside in order to find lodging two brothers of Reading carrying back the hand of blessed James which King Henry II had had brought to him as he was about to cross the Channel, that he might worship it in votive devotion and be fortified by the protection and blessing of the apostle's hand before he went upon the sea. The aforesaid Roger, who earlier seemed in despair and entirely without hope, was greatly encouraged by the arrival of so important a guest and, rejoicing in his heart (which he could not do in his body), he ran to meet the apostle's relics with his love (which he could not do with his feet), hoping to gain the help of faith and receive the rewards of

31. The translation of this word is uncertain - possibly either 'ball' or 'mortar'.

Qui quia multos a multis infirmitatibus per solum aque beati Iacobi gustum convaluisse noverat, quod potuit fecit et quod per se explere non sufficiebat per internuntios, scilicet domus supradicte canonicos, aquam illam salutarem postulans impetravit. De qua cum paululum gustasset, conturbata sunt et commota sunt interiora eius. Vomuit igitur statim virus quod pectori et cordi eius congestum incubabat, et statim in partibus illis alleviatus, quod diu prius non fecerat, manducavit et bibit. Itaque die postera et tertia de aqua illa gustans, omnem noxii humoris tabem de quacunque corporis parte evomuit. Sanitatem igitur per apostolicam gratiam plenariam adeptus Rading' venit, et vota que distinxerunt labia sua apostolo presolvit.

[Miracle XXVII] Ricardus de Leuns, miles manens in vico qui dicitur Wavercurt iuxta Banneburiam, filium suum adolescentulum Petrum nomine, ad invocationem sancti Iacobi de mortis faucibus recepit incolumem. Huic apostolo spirituali devotione devinctus, semel et secundo apud Galleciam limina inviserat apostolica, secundo procinctu predictum puerum habens convivium et contubernalem. Anno vero incarnationis dominice M^{o}. C^{o}. XX°. VII°. prefatus Petrus apud Wavercurt circiter dies xv. ante solempnia passionis apostolice adversa valitudine ad extrema deduc[fo. 175v]tus est. Siquidem effeto corpore corporeorum usu sublato sensuum, naturam languor languorem mors sibi subegerat, tenuem qui vix supererat alitum vendicans. Inter haec pater accurrens ex sua in apostolum devotione de eius in se presumens gratia iuvenem si per apostolum de mortis faucibus vite restitueretur, se Rading' ubi sue servantur reliquie gratias agendi gratia deducturum promisit. Nec votum eventus destituit. Confestim vite cedunt mortis vincula, sensibus sentiendi virtus restituitur, membris motus, vultui color vitalis. Et refloruit caro emortua et ex voluntate sua confessus est puer apostolo. Hec modico post festum apostoli tempore Rading' veniens, vota pro iuvenis vita soliturus, pater retulit, astipulante coniuge, iuvene iamdicto et aliis spectabilibus personis sexus promiscui testibus domesticis omni exceptione maioribus, licet patris nobilitas, etas veterana, lacrimarum ubertas, ad narrationis fidem satis superque sufficerent.

hope. And because he knew that many people had been cured of many illnesses by a mere taste of the water of blessed James, doing what he could himself and where he had not the strength acting through intermediaries, that is to say, canons of the aforesaid house, he sought and obtained the health-giving water. When he had tasted a drop of it, his insides were stirred up and set in motion. He immediately vomited up the poison which had settled in a lump on his chest and heart and as soon as these organs were relieved he ate and drank, as he had not done for a long time previously. And in this way, taking a little of the water on the following and on the third day, he vomited up from every part of his body all the filth of harmful fluid. And thus restored to perfect health by grace of the apostle, he came to Reading and performed the vows which he had promised orally to the apostle.

Note: Merton Priory, a house of Augustinian canons founded 1114, had no particular connection with Reading.

MIRACLE XXVII (1127)

Richard de Leuns, a knight living in the village of Warkworth, near Banbury, brought his son, a young man called Peter, safely back from the jaws of death by invoking St. James. Being bound in special devotion to this apostle, he had twice visited the apostle's home in Galicia, accompanied on the second journey by the said boy as comrade and fellow traveller. But in the year of the Lord's incarnation 1127, about fifteen days before the feast of the apostle's passion, the aforesaid Peter in failing health lay dying at Warkworth. Indeed, the use of physical faculties had gone from his exhausted body, weakness had replaced his natural fitness and (then) death had supplanted weakness, threatening the feeble life which barely yet remained. Meanwhile his father came quickly to him and, confident of the apostle's grace towards him, on account of his devotion to the apostle, promised that, if the youth might be restored to life out of the jaws of death by the apostle, he would take him to Reading, where the apostle's relics were kept, to render thanks. And the vow did not go unanswered. Immediately the chains of death gave way to life, the power of feeling came back to his senses, movement was restored to his limbs, and the colour of life reappeared in his face. His lifeless flesh bloomed again and of his own will the boy witnessed to the apostle's power. Not long after the feast of the apostle the father came to Reading to fulfil his vows on behalf of the young man's life and told of these things, with his wife's corroboration and with the above youth and other notable persons of both sexes as unimpeachable household witnesses, even though the father's noble character, his old age and floods of tears gave more than enough credibility to the story.

Note: Wavercurt in the Latin text is to be identified as Warkworth in Northamptonshire, just over the Oxfordshire border near Banbury (E. Ekwall,

Confiteantur ergo Domino misericordie eius et mirabilia eius filiis hominum.

The Concise Oxford Dictionary of English Place-names, 4th edn. (Oxford 1960), 498, under Warkleigh). If one can accept the date 1127, this story is proof that the Hand was in Reading Abbey's possession in Henry I's reign, but the placing of this miracle at the end of the series and the fact that no other miracle is so precisely dated cannot but raise suspicions as to the authenticity of the date.

May therefore the mercies and wonders of the Lord bear witness of Him to the sons of men.

Henry I's anniversary

This remarkable record[1] of the celebration in Reading Abbey of the eve (or vigil) of the anniversary of Henry I's death and of the anniversary day itself is contained in a small gathering of additional folios bound in at the end of a 13th-century manuscript of Guido's *Summa de Dictamine* from Westminster Abbey, now in the British Library, Additional Ms 8167.[2] Neither this text (fo. 200 r-v) nor the others entered on these folios appear to have any connection with Westminster Abbey, and how they came to be associated with this manuscript is unknown, except perhaps in so far as, with the exception of the present text, they contain examples of letter-writing. Folios 197v-199r contain several documents relating to the election of Walter of Colerne as abbot of Malmesbury in succession to Abbot Geoffrey (in 1260), and fo. 199r has a letter from Henry III to Boniface, archbishop of Canterbury, concerning the election of Walter Giffard as bishop of Bath and Wells in 1264.

The document with which we are concerned is not a full liturgical text, but rather a series of instructions, or rubrics, for the correct order of proceeding during the celebrations on these two days; and this is followed by a briefer second section containing directions for the monthly intercession for the king's soul throughout the year. The text resorts at times almost to note-form, and the sense of a few passages is not perhaps as clear as one might hope, particularly where the manuscript is damaged by a small hole, which renders the text somewhat uncertain on both sides of the folio. In these cases I have either tentatively supplied the missing letters or a suggestion of what is lost.

The most striking impression conveyed by the text is of the lavishness of the celebrations and intercession for the king not only at his anniversary, when it was at its fullest, but throughout the year. Firstly, we learn that the whole church is to be decked with the finest hangings and, after Vespers, the seats (?stalls) provided with covers. Secondly, at various points on both days the abbot and certain other monks playing leading roles in the liturgy wear copes, and we may presume that, given Reading's Cluniac observance, these would have been richly embroidered. We are told also that after Vespers on the vigil all the bells within and without the church are rung, and similarly after Matins on the anniversary day itself. The censing of the High Altar, the king's tomb, and the abbot and convent is mentioned several times, and we learn that from Vespers on the vigil until Compline on the anniversary, four candles are to burn brightly at the king's tomb, two at the head and two at the foot. The sequence of antiphons, psalms, canticles and collects for the Mass of the Dead, culminating in the commendation of the king's soul, is set out in

1. I am very grateful to Professor David Crouch for drawing my attention to this document, and to Dom Geoffrey Scott, abbot of Douai, for help in its interpretation

2. See *Medieval Libraries of Great Britain: a list of surviving books*, ed. N. R. Ker, 2nd edn., London 1964, 196. The folios concerned are 197-200.

detail, along with directions for the liturgical movements of the abbot and monks over the two days. All the priest-monks celebrate masses for the king on each day, those monks who are not in priest's orders reciting instead fifty psalms. They are all given full refection, or refreshment, with wine and extra dishes of food, the leftovers from which being added to the dole of bread and either meat or fish being given to the poor who come to the abbey at this time. The solemn liturgy and ceremonial were clearly elaborate and magnificent, worthily befitting the abbey's duty to its great founder.

The much briefer account of the liturgy celebrated every month throughout the rest of the year describes naturally less sumptuous, but still impressive, arrangements. We hear of bells ringing inside and outside the abbey church, the wearing of albs rather than copes and the celebration of the less grand morrow mass for the king. Moreover, on the second day of each month thirteen poor people are to be fed on the king's behalf in the hall (*aula*) of the monastery.

The account also provides valuable additional evidence on the location of Henry I's tomb within the abbey church. The king was buried at Reading on 5 January 1136, having died in Normandy on 1 December 1135.[3] The place of his burial and tomb do not become evident, however, until the reference in a 13th-century manuscript of Reading Abbey, now in Lambeth Palace Library, recording its location 'in the middle of the presbytery before the altar (*in medio presbiteri ante altare*).[4] This location is confirmed in broad terms by the record of an heraldic visitation of the abbey church in 1532 by Thomas Benolt, Clarenceux (King of Arms), which places it 'in the myddest of the high Quyer'.[5] The importance of this record is that it dates from shortly before the dissolution of the abbey in 1539.

The present text contains three references which further confirm the location of the tomb. On the vigil of the king's anniversary it records that the abbot, having entered the abbey choir, is to cense the High Altar and the king's tomb. On the day itself the abbot will, at one point, take his seat by the tomb on the pavement to the south side. Thirdly, and most persuasively, the offertory verse, 'Redemptor', is sung by four monks 'between the tomb and the altar' (*inter tumbam et altare*).[6] No measurements or distances are given in these notices, but the general relationship of the king's tomb and the High Altar is made abundantly clear. There can be no reasonable doubt that, at least between the late 13th century and 1532, and presumably also from the time of the original burial in 1136, the king's tomb was situated in a place of the greatest honour, the middle of the choir to the west of the High Altar.

3. *Reading Cartularies,* i. 14, n. 1, and references there cited.
4. See above, p. 2.
5. *The Visitations of Berkshire,* ed. W. H. Rylands, 2 vols., Harleian Society, vols. 56-7 (1907-8), i. 1. This is from British Library, Additional Ms 12479 fo. 39r; there is a copy made by Bartholomew Butler, York Herald (1538-1553), in Dublin, Trinity College Library, Ms 807, fo. 315r. I am grateful to Dr Adrian Ailes for the second reference.
6. See below, p. 107.

As to the form of the tomb, no information is forthcoming until 1397, when Richard II confirmed the abbey's liberties, having required the abbey as a condition of the confirmation to have the king's tomb and effigy properly repaired (*tumbam et ymaginem Henrici quondam regis Anglie... et fundatoris abbatie predicte in eadem humati ... honeste facerent reparari*).[7] This makes it quite clear that by this time the tomb incorporated an effigy of the king, which was probably recumbent and rested on a raised rectangular tomb-chest, as, for example, the royal tombs of the 13th and 14th centuries in Westminster Abbey. If so, it may have resembled the arrangement of King John's tomb still surviving in Worcester Cathedral, although there, while the royal effigy is of *c.* 1230, the tomb-chest dates only from *c.* 1529.

Finally, this record contains nice links with the schedule of feasts and anniversaries at Reading listed in the Worcester College manuscript.[8] Both on the vigil and on the anniversary itself, according to the present document, the monks have refection of seven extra dishes 'as on the Lord's Nativity'. This tallies precisely with the seven extra dishes which are prescribed for the celebration of this feast at Reading, as listed among the 'principal double feasts' in the Worcester College manuscript.[9] Moreover, the same manuscript shows that among the meals which the chamberlain of the abbey was to provide were those both on the vigil and on the anniversary of Henry I.[10]

7. *Reading Cartularies,* i. 107-8, no. 116.
8. Edited elsewhere in this volume, below, pp. 114-125.
9. See below, p. 115.
10. See below, p. 123.

Henry I's Anniversary

[*fo. 200r*]

[Q]uod[a] specialitatis fit in abbatia Radingie pro anima regis Henrici fundatoris illius loci.

[D]e anniversario Regis Henrici fundatoris nostri ad cuius recitationem et absolucionem que utroque die facienda est. Omnes adesse debent qui aliquo modo possunt, et ad 'Verba mea' post capitulum in choro. Lectis in capitulo que ordine cotidiano legi solent, recitatur tabula officii pro defuncto scripta sicut in dupplicibus festis. Ad Invitatorium, quod est 'Circumdederunt', quatuor fratres in [cappi]s[b] notantur. Ad tercium responsorium quatuor, ad sextum quinque, ad nonum sex. Tota ecclesia melioribus pallis ornanda est, et ante orationem Vesperorum forme operientur bankalibus. Post Vesperas, sonantibus omnibus signis deintus et deforis, et domino abbate cum cappa chorum ingresso, incipiet ebdomadarius Antiphonam 'Placebo'. Dompnus abbas, incepta Antiphona ad 'Magnificat', incensabit maius altare tantum et tumbam Regis cum duobus in cappis ad hoc assignatis, qui circa finem tercii[c] psalmi intrabunt chorum cum turribilis, qui post incensacionem altaris et tumbe pergunt incensaturi dominum abbatem. Duas ad complend' collectas dicit abbas stando et cum tono, videlicet 'Presta[d] domine quesumus' et 'Fidelium'. Ab incepcione 'Placebo' usque in crastinum post completorium ardebunt iugitur quatuor cerei ad tumbam, duo ad capud et duo ad pedes, preter alios qui ad omne officium accendentur, sicut in festis principalibus. Finitis matutin(alibus) regalibus cum appendiciis suis, et pulsatis omnibus signis deintus et deforis, intrent predicti quatuor cappis indutis, incipientes Invitatorium 'Quod est circumdederunt', ubi loco 'Glorie' dicent 'Requiem eternam'. Cetera omnia sicut in tabula notata dicentur. Ad secundam, quintam et octavam lectionem incensabitur altare et tumba et conventus sicut in festis precipuis.

a. *Letters in square brackets supplied.*
b. *Missing letters owing to hole in Ms; suggested reading.*
c. tercii *repeated in Ms.*
d. *Suggested reading.*

Henry I's Anniversary

What particularly is done in the abbey of Reading for the soul of King Henry the founder of that place.
Concerning the anniversary of King Henry, our founder, the things that are to be performed on the two days at his commemoration and absolution. All ought to be present who in any way can be, and at 'Verba mea'[11] after chapter in the choir. After the things have been read out in the chapter that are customarily read in the daily order, the table of the office composed for the dead is recited, as on double feasts. At the invitatory, which is 'Circumdederunt',[12] four brethren in [copes] are designated. At the third responsory four, at the sixth five, at the ninth six. The entire church is to be adorned with the finest hangings, and before the prayer of Vespers the seats are to be provided with covers. After vespers, with all bells ringing inside and outside, and the lord abbot with cope having entered the choir, the hebdomadary[13] shall begin the antiphon 'Placebo'.[14] The lord abbot, after the antiphon at 'Magnificat' has begun, will cense the High Altar and the king's tomb with two in copes assigned for this, who at the end of the third psalm will enter the choir with censers, and after the censing of the altar and tomb shall proceed to cense the lord abbot. The abbot says the two collects at Compline, standing and intoning, that is, 'Presta domine quesumus[15] and 'Fidelium'.[16] From the beginning of 'Placebo' until after Compline the next day four candles shall burn brightly at the tomb, two at the head and two at the feet, apart from the others which are lit at every office, as on the principal feasts. Once the royal Matins with additions has finished, and with all bells ringing inside and out, the aforesaid four persons wearing copes shall enter beginning the invitatory, which is 'Circumdederunt',[17] where in place of the 'Gloria' they shall say 'Requiem eternam'. All the other things set down in the table are said. At the second, fifth and eighth lesson the altar will be censed, as will the tomb and the convent as on the principal feasts.

11. The opening of the introit to the Mass, Psalm 5, vv. 2-4 in the Vulgate and Book of Common Prayer: 'Verba mea auribus percipe Domine'.
12. The invitatory is the psalm used to begin the office; for the text, see note 17.
13. The monk appointed for the week to lead the chapter mass and the recitation of the canonical hours.
14. From Psalm 114, verse 9, in the Vulgate (116, v. 9 in Book of Common Prayer): 'Placebo Domino in regione vivorum'.
15. Probably 'Presta Domine quesumus', a prayer for the absolution of the soul.
16. 'Fidelium anime, per misericordiam dei, requiescant in pace', a prayer for souls in Purgatory.
17. From Psalm 17, vv. 6-7 in the Vulgate (16, vv. 3-4 in the Book of Common Prayer): 'Circumdederunt me dolores mortis …'.

Post repeticionem noni responsorii. sequuntur duo psalmi consueti et due collecte premise que tunc non cum tono set indirectum dicentur. Et tunc, pulsatis omnibus signis sicut prius prenotatum est, incipitur ab ebdomadario 'Exultabunt'. Circa principium cantici 'Ego dixi' exeat dompnus abbas ad revestiendum se et etiam duo qui ei sociabuntur in cappis. Et ad 'Laudate dominum in sanctis eius' redeat ad [fo. 200v] stallum suum dompnus abbas revestitus et cum eo socii eius, qui incensare debent sicut predictum est altare et tumbam. In capitulo dicto versu et facta absolucione consueta, iterum fiet absolucio. Post Sextam vero statim pulsatur classicum donec abbas et totus conventus revestientur. Post classicum vero ingrediatur abbas ad sedile suum iuxta tumbam super pavimentum ex parte australi, associato sibi priore [si .....][e] vel alius prelatus non interfuerit. Et tunc incepto ab armario responsorio, 'Subvenite', integre fiet anime commendacio cum antiph(onis), psalmis et collectis consuetis cum conventu revestito. Novem regent chorum. responsorium a quatuor cantatur, tractus vero a sex. Omnes facient offerendam, versus offerende Redemptor a quatuor inter tumbam et altare canetur. Omnes sacerdotes tam in vigilia quam in die missas pro eo celebrent, ceteri duas quinquagenas. Refectionem plenariam sicut in natale Domini habent cum vii. ferculis plenis, quia quod residuum fuerit in usus pauperum cedere debet, et caritatem de vino tam in vigilia quam in die. Omnes pauperes ipso die supervenientes habebunt panem et carnem vel piscem, scilicet singuli singulos panes et singulas porciones de carne vel pisce.

e. Suggested reading; other letters missing owing to hole in Ms.

After the repetition of the ninth responsory there follow the two customary psalms and the two aforesaid collects, which at this time are said not by intoning but spoken; and then, with all the bells ringing as previously noted, the 'Exultabunt'[18] is begun by the hebdomadary. Around the beginning of the canticle 'Ego dixi',[19] the lord abbot and those accompanying him shall withdraw to re-vest themselves in copes. And at 'Laudate dominum in sanctis eius'[20] the lord abbot shall return to his stall, re-vested, and with him his fellows, who are to cense the altar and the tomb, as stated previously. On the return to the said chapter, and the customary absolution having been made, the absolution shall be pronounced again. And immediately after Sext[21] a peal of bells is rung until the abbot and the whole convent are re-vested. And after the peal of bells the abbot is to proceed to his seat by the tomb upon the pavement to the south side, associated with the prior [if ……] or another prelate should not be present.[22] And then, after the precentor[23] has started the responsory, 'Subvenite',[24] the commendation of the soul will be fully carried out with the customary antiphons, psalms and collects, with the convent re-vested. Nine rule the choir. The responsory is sung by four, and the tract by six. All are to do the offertory chant, the verse of the offertory 'Redemptor'[25] shall be sung by four between the tomb and the altar. All priests, both on the vigil and on the day, shall celebrate masses for him, the remainder[26] two sets of fifty psalms. They have full refection as on the Lord's Nativity with seven full extra dishes, because what is left over ought to go for the benefit of the poor,[27] and a measure of wine both on the vigil and on the day. All the poor coming on that day will have bread and meat or fish, namely, each person having bread and a single portion of meat or fish.

18. From Psalm 149, vv. 5-7 in the Vulgate and Book of Common Prayer: 'Exultabunt sancti in Gloria…..'.
19. The canticle is taken from Isaiah, 38, vv. 10-20, beginning 'Ego dixi in dimidio dierum meorum'.
20. Psalm 150 in the Vulgate and Book of Common Prayer 'Praise the Lord in his saints'.
21. The monastic office.
22. The missing word is perhaps 'episcopus' (bishop).
23. The Latin 'armarius' principally means 'librarian', but in many Benedictine houses the librarian was also the precentor, which is probably the sense intended here.
24. 'Subvenite sancti dei ….', from the Mass for the Dead.
25. The offertory is the offering of bread and wine for the Mass.
26. That is, those monks not in priest's orders.
27. This refers to the monastic dole of unconsumed food put out for the poor at the abbey gate.

De his que per annum fiunt in communi pro anima eiusdem regis.

Kl' singulorum mensium quam cicius poterit, sit pro eo officium statim post capitulum, pulsatis deforis et deintus omnibus signis, et missa matutinalis. In crastino tamen responsorium in albis et eo die tredecim pauperes in aula pro eo reficientur. Collectam habet propriam et singularem ad omnia officia defunctorum a Septuagesima usque ad kl' Novembris, sequenti die post xii. lectiones missam habet matutinalem. Et ad 'Exultabunt' prima collecta pro eo dicitur. In Rogacionibus, ad 'Exultabunt' et ad 'Placebo' primam habet collectam. Ad Rasuram semper 'Placebo' dicitur pro eo. Ad omnes missas tam in conventu quam privatas, collectam habet propriam.[f]

f. End of folio, any following folio missing.

Concerning the things that are done through the year in common for the soul of the same king.

On the first of each month as soon as possible there shall be the office for him immediately after chapter, with all the bells ringing outside and in, and the morrow mass.[28] On the next day, moreover, the responsory in albs, and on that day thirteen poor people are to be fed for him in the hall. He has the proper and particular collect for every office of the dead from Septuagesima[29] to November 1; on the following day, after twelve lessons, he has the morrow mass. And at 'Exultabunt'[30] the first collect is said for him. On Rogation Days, at 'Exultabunt' and at 'Placebo'[31] he has the first collect. At the shaving of the tonsure, 'Placebo' is always said for him. At all masses, both in the convent and private, he has the proper collect.

28. The first of two masses celebrated daily in a monastery.
29. Third Sunday before Ash Wednesday.
30. See note 18.
31. See note 14.

Feasts and Anniversaries

Schedule of feasts, anniversaries and pittances in Reading Abbey in the later thirteenth century

The same manuscript which contains the third set of Reading Abbey annals also has a very interesting and valuable list of the feasts and anniversaries observed annually in the abbey, along with information on the amounts and types of extra food and drink, or pittances, permitted to the monks on these occasions. The feasts are categorised into a series of groups according to their rank, and for each group details of the pittances are given with, in a few cases, the extra ceremonial involved in their observance.[1] The text is written in a late 13th-century hand, mainly in black ink, with the rubrics in red ink. The composition of these lists can be dated to the time of Abbot Robert of Burgate (1269-1290), since, while he and both his parents are included, no later abbot of Reading is mentioned.[2]

The value of these lists is mainly three-fold. Firstly, they reveal which feasts were regarded at Reading as most important in the lives of the monks and observed with the most generous allowances. This is followed, secondly, by a series of other groups which, though still of great importance, are marked by gradually less elaborate allowances. In each of these categories, when the feasts fall during Lent in any particular year, the pittances are accordingly less generous.[3]

Thirdly, there are five lists of deceased persons, for the celebration of whose anniversaries special extra meals are provided each year. The first two of these lists are the most substantial – in one group the sub-prior of the monastery is the provider, in the other, rather larger group it is the chamberlain. The final three lists are very much shorter and concern the cellarer, the sacrist and, with only one meal to provide, the granger. All these obedientiaries would have financed the meals out of the endowment of their obediences, but perhaps in some cases (how many is unknown) the funds would have been provided by donors. These lists are of the utmost significance as indicating those individuals whose anniversaries the monks wished, or in some cases were obliged, to observe and on which special intercession and prayer for the souls of these individuals would be made. Lastly, there is a calculation of the total number of occasions per year on which the chamberlain and the other obedientiaries had to provide wine for these celebrations.

1. Below, p. 115. For an introduction to monastic pittances, see D. Knowles, *The Monastic Order in England* (Cambridge 1940), 463-4; for the situation at Westminster Abbey, see B. Harvey, *Living and Dying in England 1100-1540* (Oxford 1993), 10-11, 43-4.
2. Below, p. 120.
3. Below, p. 115.

Two points regarding these lists can usefully be made. Firstly, for two lists the total given at the head of each is not matched by the number of items listed: thus, the list of 28 feasts called 'in special copes' contains in fact 27 items, while the list of 9 feasts called 'in simple copes' has only 8 items.[4] Whether these anomalies are due to faulty counting or whether in each case an item has been inadvertently omitted by the scribe is impossible to tell. Secondly, the sequence of names in each of the lists of deceased persons appears to follow the order of their obits each year.[5] So, for example, the first name in the chamberlain's list is that of Abbot Roger, who died January 20, followed by Abbot Anscher, who died 27 January, Abbot Reginald, died 3 February, Abbot Joseph, died 8 February, and so on for many more abbots and others. Again, the first name in the sub-prior's list is that of Abbot Richard of Chichester, who died 22 March, followed by Abbot Richard Bannister, who died after 11 July, and later in the list come Roger Bigod (earl of Norfolk), died 28 July, and Giles of Bridport, bishop of Salisbury, died 13 December. Virtually every abbot of Reading from the foundation to 1290 is included, although two appear with the title and rank which they went on to hold in other institutions, namely, Hugh, archbishop (of Rouen), formerly first abbot of Reading, and Hugh, abbot of Cluny, formerly eighth abbot.[6] It is striking, however, and as yet unexplained, that one abbot, William, called the Templar (1165-73), who became archbishop of Bordeaux (1173-87), is not included in any of these lists.

These lists provide what one might describe as a snapshot of the practices observed by the monks of Reading in the late thirteenth century and they relate to that period alone. Other feasts and anniversaries were no doubt added in the later Middle Ages, but of these we have no similarly comprehensive record. We know, however, of an important individual example from the end of 1284. On 30 December, in a long charter, the abbot and convent granted to Ela Longespée, countess of Warwick, who died in 1298, that among other things they and their successors would receive every Sunday in perpetuity 'one good and abundant pittance to the honour of the Holy Trinity' for the soul of the countess, this to be funded out of the 210 marks received from the wardship of the manor of Shenstone (Staffordshire), which the monks have by her gift.[7] Occasionally, too, additional information

4. Below, pp. 117-119.
5. The obits of abbots of Reading are given in the calendar in the 13th-century cartulary of the almoner of Reading Abbey (British Library, Cotton ms Ev), fos. 11v-16v. Two months of another calendar are contained in the 13th-century Reading manuscript which also has, among many other gems, the famous text and music of *Sumer is icumen in* (British library, Harley ms 978, fos. 15v-16r); the only difference between the obits of the first five abbots in both calendars is that Abbot Roger's in Cotton Vespasian Ev is 20 January, while in Harley 978 it is 19 January.
6. Below, p. 123.
7. British Library, Additional Charter 19633; cf British Library, Cotton ms Ev, fo. 59v. The monks' charter contains a reminder that Reading Abbey still at this date had its dependent priory at May in Scotland: it states that, to sustain the pittance in perpetuity, it allocates to the cellarer

from other sources serves to amplify that given in these lists. Thus, among the meals provided by the sub-prior, those for the souls of Abbot Robert of Burgate and his father (Nigel) and mother, Felicia,[8] can be traced to a later 13th-century list of tenants in Sheffield (in Burghfield, Berkshire) who pay rents to the sub-prior to provide meals for their souls.[9] In addition to their primary purpose, the lists yield incidentally other snippets of information of which we should otherwise be unaware, including, for example, the names of Abbot Elias's mother and father, Adam and Mary.[10] The three references to 'ale of Cholsey' are also interesting, suggesting that the monks had a special brewery at their important manor of Cholsey.[11]

of the abbey 10 marks of the 16 marks that the monks receive annually from 'our priory of May in Scotland'.

8. Below, p. 121.
9. *Reading Cartularies*, ii. 65.
10. Below, p.123.
11. Below, p. 119.

Feasts and Anniversaries

[*p. 7, col. 1*]
Memorandum quod novem sunt festa in quibus conventus debet habere brachinellos et vinum. Et dicuntur ista festa duplicia principalia. Debet autem conventus habere in eisdem festis vii. fercula; ita ut primum sint fladones, ultimum cornes. Et sunt hec:
Annuntiatio domini [a]in Quadragesima Wastell(os)[a]
Dedicatio ecclesie in Quadragesima. Wast(ellos)
Dies Pasche
Dies Pentecost'
Petri et Pauli
Sancti Jacobi apostoli
Assumptio sancte Marie
Natal(e) domini
Johannis ewangeliste

Item sunt alia ix. festa per annum que habent processionem per claustrum sicut et priora; in quibus conventus debet habere wastellos et vinum et vi. fercula; ita ut primum sint losenges vel fladones, ultimum russoles. Et sunt hec:
Epiphania domini
Purificatio sancte Marie
Ascensio domini
Philippi et Jacobi
Johannis baptiste
Sancte Trinitatis
Nativitas sancte Marie
[*col. 2*]
Festum reliquiarum
Festum omnium sanctorum.

Sunt etiam alie festivitates per annum xvi. Sine processione, que duplices secundarii dicuntur; in quibus conventus habet fabas albas et duo fercula et generale de piscibus et vinum et russoles per totum. Que tales sunt:
Festum sancti Benedicti in Quadragesima

a-a. Interlined.

Feasts and Anniversaries

[*p. 7, col. 1*]
Memorandum that there are 9 feasts on which the convent is due to have ?malted loaves[12] and wine. And these are called principal double feasts. They are also due to have on the same feasts 7 extra dishes,[13] such that the first shall be flans, the last *cornes*.[14] And these are they:
Annunciation of the Lord [25 March], in Lent wastel-breads
Dedication of the church [18 April], in Lent wastel-breads
Easter Day
Day of Pentecost
Of Peter and Paul [29 June]
Of St James the apostle [25 July]
Assumption of St Mary [15 August]
Nativity of the Lord [25 December]
Of John the Evangelist [27 December]

Item there are another 9 feasts through the year which have a procession through the cloister, as also do the first group; in which the convent is due to have wastel-breads and wine and 6 extra dishes, the first being lozenges[15] or flans, the last rissoles.[16] And these are they:
Epiphany of the Lord [6 January]
Purification of St Mary [2 February]
Ascension of the Lord
Of Philip and James [the Less] [1 May]
Of John the Baptist [24 June]
Of the Holy Trinity
Nativity of St Mary [8 September]
[*col. 2*]
Feast of relics
Feast of All Saints [1 November].

There are another 16 feasts through the year without procession, which are called secondary double; in which the convent has white beans and two extra dishes, and a normal dish[17] of fish, and wine and rissoles throughout. And such are they:
Feast of St Benedict in Lent [21 March]

12. The meaning of *brachinellos* is not entirely clear.
13. In honour of the feasts, usually of meat or fish.
14. Meaning unclear.
15. Presumably from their shape.
16. Made of minced fruits, sugar and spices, or of minced meat and spices.
17. For the Latin *generale* (plural *generalia*), a 'general' (plural 'generals'), here translated as 'normal dish', see B. Harvey, *Living and Dying in England 1100-1540* (Oxford 1993), 10-11, 43.

Inventio sancte Crucis
Marie Salome
Advincula sancti Petri
Transfiguratio domini
Exaltatio sancte Crucis
Sancti Michaelis archangeli
Sancti Martini
Sancti Andree
Conceptio sancte Marie
Stephani prothomartiris
Thome archiepiscopi
Dominica palmarum
Secunda dies Pasche
Secunda dies Pentecost'
Secunda dies Assumptionis.

Item sunt xxviii. festivitates per annum que dicuntur in cappis precipuis; in quibus conventus habet fabas albas, unum ferculum et generale de piscibus; et de russoll' quantum possit sufficere ad medietatem conventus. Et sunt hec:
[*p. 8, col. 1*]
Circumcisio domini
Vincentii martiris
Conversio sancti Pauli
Cathedra sancti Petri
Gregorii pape
Johannis ante portam Latinam
Pancratii martiris
Augustini Anglorum apostoli
Commemor(atio) sancti Pauli. [a]Russoles per tot(um).[a]
Oct(ave) apostolorum Petri et Pauli
Translatio Thome martiris
Translatio sancti Benedicti
Marie Magdalene
Oct(ave) sancti Jacobi
Sancti Laurentii martiris
Oct(ave) Assumptionis
Mathei apostoli et ewang(eliste)
Oct(ave) reliquiarum
Quintini martiris
Edmundi archiepiscopi
Katerine virginis et martiris

a-a. In red ink.

Invention of the Holy Cross [3 May]
Of Mary Salome [22 October]
St Peter Advincula [1 August]
Transfiguration of the Lord [6 August]
Exaltation of the Holy Cross [14 September]
Of St Michael the archangel [29 September]
Of St Martin [11 November]
Of St Andrew [30 November]
Conception of St Mary [8 December]
Stephen the protomartyr [26 December]
Thomas [Becket] the archbishop [of Canterbury] [29 December]
Palm Sunday
Second day of Easter
Second day of Pentecost
Second day of the Assumption [16 August].

Item there are 28 feasts through the year, which are called 'in special[18] copes', on which the convent is due to have white beans, one extra dish and a normal dish of fish; and of rissoles as much as can suffice for half the convent. And they are these:
[*p. 8, col. 1*]
Circumcision of the Lord [1 January]
Of Vincent the martyr [22 January]
Conversion of St Paul [25 January]
Of St Peter ad Cathedra [22 February]
Of Gregory [I] the pope [12 March]
Of John before the Latin Gate [6 May]
Of Pancras the martyr [12 May]
Of Augustine the apostle of the English [26 May]
Commemoration of St Paul [30 June]; rissoles throughout
Octave of the apostles Peter and Paul [6 July]
Translation of Thomas [Becket] the martyr [7 July]
Translation of St Benedict [11 July]
Of Mary Magdalene [22 July]
Octave of St James [1 August]
Of St Laurence the martyr [10 August]
Octave of the Assumption [22 August]
Of Matthew apostle and evangelist [21 September]
Octave of relics
Of Quintin the martyr [31 October]
Of Edmund [of Abingdon] the archbishop [of Canterbury] [16 November]
Of Katherine virgin and martyr [25 November]

18. That is, festal.

Nicholai episcopi
Translatio sancti Jacobi
Tercia dies Pasche
Oct(ave) Pasche
Tercia dies Pentecost'
Tercia dies Assumptionis.
In omibus festis predictis datur vinum ad prandium, et itur ad caritatem post collationem.

Sunt alie ix. festivitates que dicuntur cappe simplices. Que tales sunt:
[col. 2]
Marcelli pape et martiris
Barnabe apostoli
Symonis et Jude
Thome apostoli
Innocentium
Quartus dies Pasche
Quartus dies Pentecost'
Quartus dies Assumptionis.
In istis datur cervisia de Chauseya, nec itur ad caritatem post collationem nisi de gratia.

Item sunt quatuor dies dominici per annum in quibus datur cervisia de Chauseya:
Dominica prima Adventus
Dominica Septuagesima
Dominica prima Quadragesime
Dominica medie Quadragesime.
[a] Set in his sit caritas et in omnibus dominicis Adventus et Quadragesime.[a]

Supprior facit per annum xi. refectiones, videlicet:
Pro Ricardo abbate Cycestr' [b]de tribus marcis et dimidia[b]
Pro Ricardo abbate Banastr'
Pro Rogero decano Leom(inistrie) [b]de Chaus(eya)[b]
Pro Huberto decano Leom(inistrie)
Pro Rogero Bigod

a-a. In red ink.
***b-b**. Added in the same hand.*

Of Nicholas the bishop [6 December]
Translation of St James
Third day of Easter
Octave of Easter
Third day of Pentecost
Third day of the Assumption [17 August].
On all the said feasts wine is given at lunch, and it goes to *caritas*[19] after collation.[20]

There are another 9 feasts which are called 'in simple copes'. And such are they:
[*col. 2*]
Of Marcellus, pope and martyr [16 January]
Of Barnabas the apostle [11 June]
Of Simon and Jude [28 October]
Of Thomas the apostle [21 December]
Of the [Holy] Innocents [28 December]
Fourth day of Easter
Fourth day of Pentecost
Fourth day of the Assumption [18 August].
On these ale of Cholsey is given, and it does not go to the *caritas* after collation, except by grace.

Item there are four Sundays through the year on which ale of Cholsey is given:
First Sunday of Advent
Septuagesima Sunday
First Sunday of Lent
Sunday of mid-Lent.
But on these there is to be *caritas* and on all Sundays of Advent and Lent.

The sub-prior provides meals through the year, namely:
For Abbot Richard of Chichester [1238-62], of three and a half marks
For Abbot Richard Bannister [1262-69]
For Roger, dean of Leominster,[21] of Cholsey
For Hubert, dean of Leominster[22]
For Roger Bigod, [earl of Norfolk, 1189-1221][23]

19. Probably an allowance of food or drink.
20. A light refreshment before retiring to bed.
21. Possibly either dean, or prior, of Leominster priory or rural dean of Leominster
22. Hubert, dean/prior of Leominster occurs importantly in the annal for 1255 in the 3rd set of Reading annals (above, p. 45).
23. A benefactor to the abbey (*Reading Cartularies*, i. 221-4, 371); according to his obit in the Reading Abbey calendar, he died 28 July (British Library, Cotton ms Vespasian Ev, fo.14v).

Pro Thoma de Osen' decano Leom(inistrie) [a]de tribus marcis[a]
Pro Rogero de Liford
Pro Egidio episcopo Sar'
Pro patre domini Roberti abbatis de Burg'
Pro Felicia matre eiusdem abbatis
Pro domino Roberto abbate de Burg'
[b]Pro Osberto decano Leom(inistrie)[b]

[*p. 9, col. 1*]
Hec sunt refectiones quas facit camerarius:
Pro Rogero abbate
Pro Anschero abbate
Pro Reginaldo abbate
Pro Joseph abbate
Pro Symone abbate
Pro Brientio filio comitis
Pro Adeliza de Yveri
Pro Adeliza regina
Pro Adam abbate
Pro Hugone Herefordensi episcopo
Pro Nichol(ao) de la ruge
Pro professis nostris et ad succurr(endum)
Pro Matilde regina
Pro Willelmo marescallo
Pro David rege Scotie

a-a. Added in the same hand.
b-b. Deleted.

For Thomas of Osney, dean of Leominster,[24] of three marks
For Roger de Liford[25]
For Giles [of Bridport], bishop of Salisbury [1257-62]
For the father of lord abbot Robert of Burgate
For Felicia, mother of the same abbot
For lord abbot Robert of Burgate [1269-90]
For Osbert, dean of Leominster[26]

[p. 9, col. 1]
These are the meals which the chamberlain provides:
For abbot Roger [1158-65]
For abbot Anscher [1130-35]
For abbot Reginald [1154-58]
For abbot Joseph [1173-86]
For abbot Simon [1213-26]
For Brian Fitz Count[27]
For Adeliza d'Ivry[28]
For Queen Adeliza[29]
For abbot Adam [of Lathbury, 1226-38]
For Hugh [de Mapenore], bishop of Hereford [1216-19][30]
For Nicholas de la ruge
For our professed [monks] and ad succurrendum
For Queen Matilda[31]
For William Marshal[32]
For David, king of Scotland [1124-53][33]

24. Possibly a hitherto unrecorded dean, or prior, of Leominster.
25. Probably Roger de Lilford, prior of Leominster, who occurs on two occasions with former prior Hubert (*Heads of Religious Houses: England and Wales, II, 1216-1377*, ed. D. M. Smith and V.C.M. London (Cambridge 2001), 117).
26. He occurs, probably as rural dean of Leominster, in the second half of the 12th century (B. R. Kemp, 'Hereditary Benefices in the Medieval Church: a Herefordshire Example', *Bulletin of the Institute of Historical Research*, xliii, 1970, 9-10).
27. Of Wallingford, he occurs as a staunch supporter of the Angevin cause and in the apparent role of patron, or protector, of Reading Abbey during the troubles of Stephen's reign, c. 1141-51 (*Reading Cartularies*, ii. 5-6, 345).
28. Donor of Rowington (Warwickshire) to the abbey, c. 1133 (*ibid*, i. 448-9).
29. Second wife and widow of Henry I, donor of Aston (Hertfordshire) in 1136 (*ibid*, i. 301-04).
30. The bishop of Hereford who confirmed Reading Abbey's control of Leominster Priory in 1216-18 (*Reading Cartularies*, i. 293-4) after the bitter dispute with bishop Giles de Braose (see pp. 12, 19-21).
31. First wife of Henry I who died in 1118.
32. The great William Marshal, earl of Pembroke (died at Caversham in 1219), whose body rested for a day in the chapel he had built in Reading Abbey (*Reading Cartularies*, ii. 226; and see the earl's obit, 14 May, in the Reading Abbey calendar, British Library, Cotton ms Vespasian Ev, fo. 13v).
33. A major benefactor to the abbey, especially with his gift of what became the priory of May in Scotland (*Reading Cartularies*, ii. 345 ff.).

Pro Willelmo de Huntercumbe et c^s^
Pro H(enrico) ii^o^ filio M(atildis) Imperatricis
Pro Radulfo priore
Pro patribus nostris
Pro Rogero decano de Chaus(eya)
Prp matribus nostris
Pro Hugone de Mortuo mari
Pro Johanne rege
Pro Hugone archiepiscopo
Pro Alboldo et Ingelram
Pro Henrico rege fundatore, in vigilia et in die
Pro Edwardo abbate
Pro Osberto decano.

Cellararius faciet v. refectiones preter regulam:
[*col. 2*]
Pro Helya abbate cum wastell(is)
Pro Hugone abbate Cluniac' de ii. mar(cis) et di(midia)
Pro Adam patre Hel(ye) abbatis
Item pro Maria matre eiusdem de redditu de Sewelle
Pro Warino granetar(io)
Item quando legitur Regula.

Sacrista faciet duas refectiones:
Pro Gervasio sacrista, post sanctum Vincentium
Pro Lamberto, ad rasuram ante Natale.

For William of Huntercombe
For King Henry II [1154-89], son of the Empress Matilda[34]
For prior Ralph
For our fathers
For Roger, dean of Cholsey[35]
For our mothers
For Hugh de Mortimer[36]
For King John [1199-1216][37]
For Hugh [of Amiens], archbishop [of Rouen, 1130-64][38]
For Albold and Ingelram [Apostolicus][39]
For the vigil and the day of King Henry [I] the founder [30 November and 1 December]
For abbot Edward [1136-*c.*1154]
For Osbert the dean[40]

The cellarer is to provide 5 meals, beyond the Rule:
[*col. 2*]
For Abbot Elias [1200-1213], with wastel-breads
For Hugh [V], abbot of Cluny [1199-1207], formerly abbot of Reading 1186-1199], of 2½ marks
For Adam, father of Abbot Elias
Item, for Mary, mother of the same, out of the rent of Showell [in Little Tew, Oxfordshire)].[41]
For Warin the granger
Item, when the Rule is read.

The sacrist is to provide two meals:
For Gervase the sacrist, after St Vincent
For Lambert, at the shaving of the tonsure before Christmas.

34. Henry II recovered the Hand of St James for the abbey and gave the annual fair of St James, as well as an annual payment of 40 marks out of the king's rents in Hoo (Kent), which under King John was converted into an assignment of land there (*Reading Cartularies*, i. 56-7, 321-4).
35. Probably an early monastic dean of the Cluniac type, in charge of Reading's manor of Cholsey.
36. Either Hugh de Mortimer (d. 1180 x 81), who gave properties in Stratfield Mortimer (Berks) and Headbourne Worthy (Hants) in c.1170 x 73, or Hugh, his son, who died in his father's lifetime and was buried in the abbey, and who gave further properties in these places (*ibid*, ii. 232-4).
37. Generous benefactor and friend of Reading Abbey (see p. 5).
38. First abbot of Reading, 1123-30; not otherwise mentioned in these lists.
39. Donors, respectively, of How End, in Houghton Conquest (Bedfordshire), and Whitsbury (Hampshire, formerly Wiltshire) (*Reading Cartularies*, i. 200, 250-1).
40. Probably rural dean of Leominster (see the deleted reference in the preceding list).
41. For Reading Abbey's possessions in Showell, see *Reading Cartularies*, i. 392 ff.

Granetarius faciet unam refectionem, scilicet kl' Octobris:
Pro professis et parentibus et benefactoribus , et pro Andrea granetario.

Summa dierum in quibus camer(arius) inveniet vinum per annum:
Pro festis, lxxii
Pro refectionibus, xxix
Summa totalis quoad camerar(ius), iiii^{xx} xi.

Item xi. vina de suppriore.
Item v. de cellarario, excepta regula.
Item ii. de sacrista.
Item unum de granetario.
Summa omnium vinorum per annum, C. et x.

The granger is to provide 1 meal, that is, on 1 October:
For [our] professed monks, parents and benefactors, and for Andrew the granger.

Total of days on which the chamberlain is to provide wine through the year:
For feasts, 72
For meals, 29.
Sum total as regards the chamberlain, 91.

Item, 11 wines of the sub-prior.
Item, 5 of the cellarer, in exception to the Rule.
Item, 2 of the sacrist.
Item, 1 of the granger.

Sum total of all wines through the year, 110.

Index to persons and places

Abingdon, abbey of (Benedictine), 39; abbot of, *see* Blosmevile, John de; Luke; Newbury, William of
Abingdon, Edmund of, archbishop of Canterbury, 35, 39, 43
Adam, prior of Reading, 23
Adeliza of Louvain, queen of England, wife/widow of Henry I, 2, 121 and n.
Ailes, Adrian, 102n.
Alan, prior of Reading, 6, 7
Albold,123 and n.
Alexander II, king of Scotland, 23 and n., 25, 29, 41; sister of, *see* Margaret; wife of, *see* Joan
Alexander III, king of Scotland, 41, 43 and n.
Alfonso VIII, king of Castile, 1, 25n.
Alfonso X, king of Castile, 43n.
Alice, girl of Essex, 69
Amiens (France), Hugh of, abbot of Reading, 112, 123n; archbishop of Rouen, 112, 123
Andelys, les (France), 8. 17
Andover (Hants),
  Alan of, 47
  Ranulf of, 49
Andrew, granger of Reading Abbey, 125
Angoulême, count of, *see* Audemar
  Isabella of, queen of England, wife of John, 17, 29
Anian, bishop of St Asaph, 43
Anscher, abbot of Reading, 3, 79n, 112, 121
Anselm, sub-prior of Reading, 71n.
Aquablanca, Peter de, bishop of Hereford, 89
Aquilina, daughter of Reginald de Courtenay and wife of Gilbert Basset, 89, 91n
Aquitaine, Eleanor of, queen of England, wife of Henry II, 19
Arches (France), castle of, 95n.
Ardington, 91n.
Arthur, count of Brittany, 19
Aston (Herts), 121n.
Audemar, count of Angoulême, 17
Avalon, Hugh of, bishop of Lincoln, 29

Baldwin, count of Flanders, 17
Banbury (Oxon), 97
Bangor (Wales), bishop of, 43
Bannister, Richard, abbot of Reading, 4, 45, 112, 119
Barking (Essex), abbey of (Benedictine nuns), 65
Basset,
  Alan, 35
  Gilbert, 35, 41
  Gilbert (*another*), 91n.; wife of, *see* Aquilina
  Philip, 51
Bath and Wells (Somerset), bishop of, *see* Giffard, Walter
Baynard's Castle (London), 25
Becket, Thomas, St, archbishop of Canterbury, 4-5, 55, 58, 85n, 87, 89n.
Beatrice, daughter of Henry III, 41
Bechamt', Peter de, 49
Bedford (Beds), castle of, 31
Benolt, Thomas, Clarenceux King of Arms, 102
Berkshire, 5, 48
Berkshire, archdeacon of, *see* Bridport , Giles of
Bermondsey (Surrey), priory of (Cluniac), annals of, 5
Berwick-on-Tweed (Berwicks), 23
Bethell, Denis, 53n.
Bicester (Oxon), priory of (Augustinian), 91n
Bigod, Bigott,
  Hugh, 47
  Roger, steward (d. 1107), 54
  Roger (*another)*, earl of Norfolk, 112, 119
Bicchieri, Guala, papal legate, 27
Bingham, Robert de, bishop of Salisbury, 7

Bishopstone (Berks or Wilts), Richard of, 49
Blewbury, Richard of, 49
Blois (France),
  Henry of, bishop of Winchester, 1, 55, 56
  William of, bishop of Lincoln, 19
  William of, bishop of Worcester, 37
Blosmevile, John de, abbot of Abingdon, 39, 45
Blundevile, Ranulph de, earl of Chester, 35
Bohun, Jocelin de, bishop of Salisbury, 59, 79n.
Boniface, archbishop of Canterbury, 101
Bordeaux (France), archbishop of, *see* William, the Templar
Boulogne (France), count of, 59, *and see* Matthew
Bouvines (France), battle of, 11
Bradfield, 81 and n.
Braggeham, Simon de, 47
Brakelond, Jocelin of, 1
Braose,
  Giles de, bishop of Hereford, 19, 22, 121n.
  Matilda de, 23
  William de, father of Giles, 21
  William de (*another*), 33
Breauté,
  Fawkes de, 31
  William de, his brother, 31
Bridport (Dorset), Giles of, archdeacon of Berks, 45; bishop of Salisbury, 6, 45, 47, 112, 121
Brindisi (Italy), 33n.
Bristol, 23, 25
  St James's priory in (Benedictine), 39
Brittany (France), 33 n.
Brittany, count of, *see* Arthur
Brochol', William de, 49
Brun, Hugh de, 19
Buckinghamshire, 58
Bucklebury, 57, 59, 77
  parish of, 79n.
  dean of (monastic), *see* Peter
  St Mary Magdalen's chapel at, 79n.
Burgate (?Hants or Surrey), Robert of, abbot of Reading, 111, 113, 121; father of, Nigel, 113, 121; mother of, Felicia, 113, 121
Burgeys, Laurence, bailiff of Reading, 10, 19, 51
Burgh, Hubert de, justiciar, 31 n., 33, 35
Burghfield, 113
Burgilun, Stephen de, 45
Bury St Edmunds (Suff), abbey of (Benedictine), 1
Butler, Bartholomew, York Herald, 102n.
Byenst', Philip de, 49

Cambridge (Cambs), St John's College, 3
Canterbury (Kent), 29, 58, 87
  St Augustine' abbey (Benedictine), abbot of, 49
  archbishop of, *see* Abingdon, Edmund of; Becket, Thomas; Boniface; Grant, Richard le; Langton, Stephen; St Augustine; Walter, Hubert
  cathedral of, monks of, 21, 39
  province of, 14
Cantilupe, Walter, bishop of Worcester, 37, 43
Castile (Spain),
  king of, *see* Alfonso III; Alfonso X
  Blanche of, 17
  Eleanor of, queen of England, 43
Caversham (Berks, formerly Oxon), bridge of, 11, 39, 85n.
  see also 'Hailesb'
Chalus-Chabrol (France), castle of, 17
Chester, earldom of, 43; earl of, *see* Blundevile, Ranulph de
Chichester (Sussex), bishop of, *see* Wyche, Richard de
Chichester, Richard of, abbot of Reading, 4, 37, 45, 112, 119
Cholsey, 113, 119
  dean of, *see* Roger
Clare,
  Gilbert de, earl of Gloucester, 33; widow of, *see* Isabella

Clare, cont
Richard de, earl of Gloucester, 47 and n.
Clerkenwell (London), 23n.
Cluny (Burgundy), 3, 10
abbey of (Cluniac), abbot of, *see* Hugh V; Pons
Colerne (Wilts), Walter of, abbot of Malmesbury, 101
Collingbourne (Wilts), 73; Collingbourne Ducis and Collingbourne Kingston, 75
Colwall (Herefs), 29
Constantinople, city of, 19
Cornwall, earl of, *see* Richard
Courtenay, Reginald, 89, 91n; daughter of, *see* Aquilina
Crevequer, William de, 54n.
Crouch, David, 101n.
Curridge, 81

Damietta, city of, 29, 43
David I, king of Scotland, 121 and n.
David, prince in Wales
Despenser,
Adelina, daughter of Philip Basset, 51
Hugh le, 51n.
Devizes (Wilts), 35
Diceto, Ralph de, 59, 95n.
Douai (Berks), abbey of (Benedictine), abbot of, *see* Scott, Dom. Geoffrey
Dover (Kent), 21, 47
Dreux, Peter of, count of Brittany, 35
Driencourt (France), castle of, 93
Dublin (Ireland), Trinity College, Library, 102n.
Dunmow (Essex), 9
Little, priory of (Augustinian), 9
Dunstable (Beds), priory of (Augustinian), annals of, 9 and n, 10, 11 n

Earley, 63
Earley, William Adam of, 51
Edmund, son of Henry III, 41
Edward I, king of England, as prince, 39, 43, 47; as king, 49;
wife of, *see* Castile, Eleanor of;
son of, *see* Henry
Edward, abbot of Reading, 123
Eleanor,
countess of Pembroke, sister of King Henry III and widow of William Marshal II, earl of Pembroke, 37 and n.
daughter of Simon de Montfort and niece of King Edward I, 49
sister of King John and wife of Alfonso VIII of Castile, 17
Elias, abbot of Reading (formerly chamberlain), 10, 17, 19, 51, 123;
father of, Adam, 113, 123;
mother of, Mary, 123
Ely (Cambs), bishop of, *see* Eustace
England, 13, 19, 21, 23, 25, 27, 31, 33, 37, 39, 41, 45, 54-5, 58, 81
king of, *see* Edward I; Henry I; Henry II; Henry III; John; Richard I; Richard II; Stephen
queen of, *see* Adeliza of Louvain; Angoulême, Isabella of; Aquitaine, Eleanor of; Castile, Eleanor of; Provence, Eleanor of
royal family of, 7
barons of, 8, 9 and n, 25, 31, 47
church of, 39
Interdict on, 10
Essex, 58; *and see* Alice
earl of, *see* Fitz Peter, Geoffrey
'Estonie', 85, 89n.
Eustace, bishop of Ely, 21, 25
Evesham (Worcs), battle of, 10, 51n.
Evesham, Silvester of, bishop of Worcester, 27

Ferentino (Italy), John of, cardinal deacon of S. Maria in Via Lata, papal legate, 19
Figheldean (Wilts), Robert of, 49
Fitz Count, Brian, of Wallingford, 54n, 121 and n
Fitz Herbert, Peter, 37
Fitz Peter, earl of Essex, 25
Fitz Walter, Robert, 8-9, 25
Flanders, 11
count of, 19, *and see* Baldwin; Philip
Matilda of, queen of England, 121 and n.

Foliot,
Gilbert, bishop of London, 59 & n.
Hugh, bishop of Hereford, 29, 37
Fontevrault (France), 17
Forns', John de, 45
Fornset', Walter de, 49
France, 11, 25, 41
king of, *see* Louis VIII; Louis IX; Philip II
Franciscans, 39
Frederick II, emperor, 7, 33, 35, 37, 39, 41, 43; as king of Jerusalem, 33; wife of, *see* Isabella
French, 27

Galicia (Spain), 97
Gascony (France), 31, 33, 41, 43
Geoffrey,
abbot of Malmesbury, 101
canon (chaplain of Robert Fitz Walter), 8, 25
Germany, 3, 8, 54-5
king of, *see* Otto IV; Richard, earl of Cornwall
Gervase, sacrist of Reading Abbey, 123
Gibuin, Ralph, 93 and n.
Giffard, Walter, bishop of Bath and Wells, 101
Gilbert, keeper of hounds, 81
Glastonbury (Som.), abbey of (Benedictine), abbot of, 49
Gloucester (Glos), 27
abbey of (Benedictine), 39; abbot of, 14, 49
cathedral of, 53
Gloucester,
earl of, 58, 73, 75n, *and see* Clare, Gilbert de; Clare, Richard de
Henry of, 47
Goda, wife of Hereward, knight of Herefordshire, 69
Goulet, Le, treaty of, 8
Grant, Richard le, archbishop of Canterbury, 33, 35
Gray, Walter de, archbishop of York, 27, 45
Gregory IX, pope (formerly Ugo, bishop of Ostia), 33, 35, 37, 39, 41
Grosseteste, Robert, bishop of Lincoln, 37
Grubbe, Walter, dean/prior of Leominster, 29; abbot of Shrewsbury, 29
Guala, papal legate, *see* Bicchieri
Guildford (Surrey), 59n.
John of, 45
Gwynedd (North Wales), prince of, *see* Llewelyn ap Iorweth

'Hailesb' (in Caversham), 29
Hardwick, Ralph of, 49
Hastings, Henry of, 47
Haver, Edward, of Reading, and daughter, 67
Havering (Essex), 39
Headbourne Worthy (Hants), 123n.
Henlow (Beds), Geoffrey of, bishop of St Davids, 19
Henry I, king of England, 1-4 6-7, 54-6. 101-3,123 and n.
Henry II, king of England, 1-2, 17, 53-6, 59, 77, 89, 93, 95n, 123 and n; mother of, *see* Matilda, Empress; son of, *see* Henry the Young king
Henry III , king of England, as prince, 19; as king, 4, 9 and n, 10, 27, 29, 31, 33, 35, 37, 39, 41, 43, 47, 101; called Henry IV, 29 and n. 152; daughter of, *see* Beatrice; Margaret; sister of, *see* Eleanor, countess of Pembroke; son of, *see* Edmund; Edward I
Henry the Young King, eldest son of Henry II, 29n.
Henry, son of King Edward I, 59n.
Henry V, Holy Roman Empereor, 55
Henry, count palatine of the Rhine, 21n.
Henry the Lion, duke of Saxony, 21 and n.
Hereford, bishop of, 12, 13, *and see* Aquablanca, Peter de; Braose, Giles de; Foliot, Hugh; Maidstone, Ralph of; Mapenore, Hugh de
Herefordshire, 58; *and see* Goda; Hereward
Hereward, knight of Herefordshire, 69

Holy Land, 7, 33
Holy Roman Emperor, *see* Frederick II; Henry V; Otto IV
Honorius III, pope, 27, 29, 33
Hoo (Kent), 123n.
Hosatus, Roger, canon of Merton Priory, 95
Houghton Conquest (Beds),
How End in, 45n, 123n.
Adam of, sub-prior of Reading, 51
Warin of, 45
How End (Beds), *see* Houghton Conquest
Howden (Yorks), Roger of, chronicler, 56
Hubert, dean/prior of Leominster, 13, 41, 45, 119 and n.
Hugh V, abbot of Cluny, 10, 17, 112, 123
Hugh I, abbot of Reading, 2-3,
Hugh II, abbot of Reading, 10, 17, 112, 123
Hugh, prior of Lewes, later Hugh I, abbot of Reading, 2-3
Huntercombe (Oxon), William of, 123
Hurry, J. B., 4

Ickham, Peter of, chronicler, 55
Ingelram (Apostolicus), 123 and n.
Innocent III, pope, 11, 14, 19n, 21, 25, 27
Innocent IV, pope, 41, 43
Ireland, 58, 91
Isabella,
daughter of King John, and wife of Emperor Frederick II, 37
widow of Gilbert de Clare, earl of Gloucester, and wife of Richard, earl of Cornwall, 35, 39, 45
Ivry, Adeliza d', 121 and n.

Jerusalem, 7, 17, 19, 33, 41; king of, *see* Frederick II
Joan, daughter of King John, and queen of Scotland, wife of Alexander II, 23 and n, 29, 39
John, king of England, 8-11, 17, 19, 21n, 94, 23, 25, 27, 29n, 54, 103, 123 and n; as prince, 5, 8, 58, 91; as Lord of Ireland, 91n; daughter of, *see* Isabella; Joan
John,
clerk, 65
fisherman, daughter of, *see* Ysembela
monk of Reading, 73
Joseph,
abbot of Reading, 4
prior of Leominster, 3

Kennet, River, 11, 35
Kent, 58, 89n.
Kildare (Ireland), 35
Kilkenny (Ireland), 35

Lacy,
Edmund de, heir to earldom of Lincoln, 45 and n.
Hugh de, lord of Ulster, 23 and n.
John de, earl of Lincoln, 39, 47n.
Margaret de, countess of Lincoln, 47
Walter de, lord of Meath, 23 and n, 41
La Marche, count of, *see* Lusignan, Hugh de
Lambert, 123
Lambeth Palace, London, library of, 1, 102
Langton, Stephen, archbishop of Canterbury, 21, 25, 29, 33
Las Navas de Tolosa (Spain), battle of, 25n.
Lathbury (Bucks), Adam of, abbot of Reading, 31, 37, 121
Lauton', Adam de, 47
Leicester, earl of, *see* Montfort, Simon of
Leominster (Herefs), 43, 47, 49
nunnery of, 3
priory of (Benedictine), 3, 12-13, 19, 39, 53, 55; dean/prior of, *see* Grubbe, Walter; Hubert; Joseph; Lilford, Roger de; Osbert; Osney, Thomas of; Roger
patron of, *see* Peter, St
Leominster,
Nicholas of, 49
Walter of, 47

Leuns, Richard de, knight, 97; son of, *see* Peter
Lewes (Sussex), priory of St Pancras of (Cluniac), 2; prior of, *see* Hugh
battle of, 4, 9, 47
Lilford, Roger de, prior of Leominster, 121 and n.
Limousin (France), 17
Lincoln,
Hugh of, 49
bishop of, *see* Avalon, Hugh of; Blois, William of; Grosseteste, Robert; Wells, Hugh of
countess of, *see* Lacy, Margaret de
earldom of, 45n; earl of, *see* Lacy, John de; William, husband of Queen Adeliza of Louvain; heir to, *see* Lacy, Edmund de
Liscombe (Bucks), 93n.
Llewelyn ap Iorwerth, Prince of Gwynedd (N. Wales), 'king of the Welsh', 23 and n, 31, 33, 39
Llewelyn ap Gruffudd, prince of Wales, 49
Loddon, River, 11, 35
London, 9, 17, 21n.92, 23, 25 and n, 37, 47, 49; Jews of, 47; Londoners, 47
bishop of, *see* Niger, Roger; Sainte-Mère-Eglise, William of
St Paul's Cathedral, 41
Tower of, 47
Longespée,
Ela, countess of Warwick, 112
William, earl of Salisbury, 11, 25, 31
Louis VIII, king of France, as prince, 17, 27; as king, 31
Louis IX, king of France, 31
Lucy, Godfrey de, bishop of Winchester, 19
Luke, abbot of Abingdon, 39
Lusignan,
Geoffrey de, 19, 45n.
Guy de, 45 and n.
Hugh de, count of La Marche, 29 and n.

Maidstone (Kent), 39
Ralph of, bishop of Hereford, 37, 39
Malcuvenant, Mauger, sheriff of Surrey, 61, 63n.
Mall', Savaric de, 19
Malmesbury (Wilts), abbey of (Benedictine), 1; abbot of, *see* Colerne, Walter of; Geoffrey
Malmesbury, William of, 1
Mapenore, Hugh de, bishop of Hereford, 29, 121 and n.
Margaret,
daughter of William I, king of Scotland and sister of Alexander II, king of Scotland, 37
daughter of Henry III, 39; queen of Scotland, 39n; wife of Alexander III, king of Scotland, 43
Marlston, 77n.
Marshal,
Gilbert, earl of Pembroke, 27, 35, 41
Richard, called Strongbow, earl of Pembroke, 35 and n.
Roger, earl (prob. erroneous), 47
Walter, earl of Pembroke, 7, 47n.
William I, earl of Pembroke (d. 1219), 29, 121 and n; daughter of, *see* Isabella, widow of Gilbert de Clare
William II, earl of Pembroke, 27 and n, 33; widow of, *see* Eleanor
Martel, Geoffrey, 77n.
Matilda, Empress, mother of King Henry II, 54-5, 123
Matthew, count of Boulogne, 93, 95n; brother of, *see* Philip, count of Flanders
Mauger, bishop of Worcester, 21
May (Scotland), priory of (Benedictine), 112n, 121n.
Mayer, Hans, 54-6, 58
Meath (Ireland), lord of, *see* Lacy, Walter de
Mediterranean, the, 7
Merton (Surrey), priory of (Augustinian), 95, 97n; canon of, 58, *and see* Hosatus, Roger
Milford Haven (Wales), 91n.
Mirebeau (France), 19
Montferrat, marquis of, 45

Montfort,
Peter de, 47
Simon de, earl of Leicester, 4, 10, 37; daughter of, *see* Eleanor; son of, Simon, 47
Mortimer, Hugh de, 123 and n.

Newark (Notts), 47
Newbury, 81n.
William of, abbot of Abingdon, 45
Niger, Roger, bishop of London, 41
Normandy (France), 8, 17, 21, 23, 102
Northampton (Northants), 8, 21, 23, 25; town and castle of, 47
Norwich (Norfolk), bishop of, *see* Raleigh, William de; bishop-elect of, *see* Pandulf
Norwich, Geoffrey of, 23, 25
Notley (Bucks), abbey of (Augustinian), abbot of, *see* Osbert; canons of, 85n.
Nottingham (Notts), 23

Osbert,
abbot of Notley, 85
dean of Leominster, 121 and n, 123
Osney (Bucks), Thomas of, dean of Leominster, 121 and n.
Ostia (Italy), bishop of, *see* Gregory IX
Othery (?Somerset), Jordan of, 47
Otto, cardinal deacon of S. Nicola in Carcere, papal legate, 37, 41; bishop of Porto, 41n.
Otto IV, king of Germany , Holy Roman Emperor, 11, 21, 23, 27
Oxford (Oxon), 45, 93; Stockwell Street in, 14, 49
Gloucester College, 14
Worcester College, 6, 14, 103
Oxford, Robert of, 45
Oxfordshire, 58

Pandulf (Verracclo), papal nuncio, 23; papal legate, 27; bishop-elect of Norwich, 29
Papal legate, *see* Bicchieri, Guala; Ferentino, John of; Otto; Pandulf; Tusculum, Nicholas of
Paris, Matthew, 2, 4-5, 55
Pembroke,
countess of, *see* Eleanor
earl of, *see* Marshal, Gilbert; Marshal, Richard; Marshal, Walter; Marshal, William I and II,
Pershore (Worcs), abbey of (Benedictine), 39
Peter,
bishop of St Asaph, 37
dean of Bucklebury (monastic), 77
prior of Reading, 2-3
son of Richard de Leuns, 97
Peter, St, patron of Leominster priory, 12, 21
Philip II, king of France, 8, 11, 17, 31
Philip, count of Flanders, 93
Poitou (France), 19, 25, 29
count of, *see* Richard, earl of Cornwall
Pons, abbot of Cluny, 2
Poore, Richard, bishop of Salisbury, 12, 29
Pope, *see* Gregory IX; Honorius III; Honorius IV
Porto (Portugal), bishop of, *see* Otto
Portsmouth (Hants), 54n.
Provence (France),
count of, 37
Eleanor of, queen of England, 37, 41
Raleigh, William de, bishop of Norwich, 41; bishop of Winchester, 41, 43
Ralph, prior (of Reading), 123
Rannulf the Chancellor, 54
Reading, 8, 9 and n, 10-11, 19, 37, 39, 45, 47, 57-9, 61, 63, 65, 69, 71, 73, 75, 81, 83, 85, 87, 89, 91, 93, 95, 97; barn at, 31; bridge of, 11, 39; *and see* Haver, Edward; Vastern; William, boy of
bailiff of, *see* Burgeys, Laurence
Franciscan friary, 10, 35; St Edmund's chapel, 10, 19, 51
Reading Abbey (Benedictine), *passim*; Benedictine chapter at, 13, 49; whirlwind and lightning strike at, 12, 14-15, 21

Reading Abbey, cont
abbot of, *see* Anscher; Bannister, Richard; Burgate, Robert of; Chichester, Richard of; Edward; Elias; Hugh I; Hugh II; Joseph; Lathbury, Adam of; Reginald; Roger; Simon; William, the Templar
cellarer of, 111, 112n, 123, 125
chamber, chamberlain of, 6, 13, 111, 121, 125
granger of. 111, 125, *and see* Andrew; Warin
infirmary of, 13
kitchen of, 13
monk of, *see* John; Thomas
precentor of, *see* Sutton, Richard of
prior of, *see* Adam; Alan; Peter
sacrist of, 111, 123, 125, *and see* Gervase
sub-prior of, 6, 111, 113, 119, 125, *and see* Anselm; Houghton Conquest, Adam of; Simon; William
Reginald, abbot of Reading, 112, 121
Rhine, count palatine of, *see* Henry
Richard I, king of England, 5-6, 17
Richard II, king of England, 103
Richard, earl of Cornwall, 23, 31, 33, 35, 37, 41, 45; count of Poitou, 33; king of Germany, 45, 47; wife of, *see* Isabella, widow of Gilbert de Clare; Sanchia
Roches,
Peter des, bishop of Winchester, 27, 33
William des, 19
Rochester (Kent),
castle of, 47
cathedral of, monks of, 39
Roger,
abbot of Reading, 112 and n, 121
dean of Cholsey, 123 and n.
dean/prior of Leominster, 119 and n.
Rome, 21, 37, 39, 41
Fourth Lateran Council at, 11, 25, 35
Rowington (Warks), 121n.
Ruge, Nicholas de la, 121
St Albans (Herts), abbey of (Benedictine), 1; abbot of, 14, 49
St Andrews (Scotland), bishop of, *see* William
St Asaph (Wales), bishop of, *see* Anian; Peter
St Augustine, archbishop of Canterbury, 'bishop of the English', 29
St Davids (Wales), bishop of, 43 *and see* Henlow, Geoffrey of
St Edmund, Thomas de, 49
St James, 58; hand of, 53-99 *passim*, 123n.
St Malo (France), 33n
St Mary Magdalen, altar of in Reading Abbey, 89
Sainte-Mère-Eglise, William of, bishop of London, 21
St Pancras, *see* Lewes
St Richard of Chichester, *see* Wyche, Richard de
St Vincent, 123
St Wulfstan, bishop of Worcester, 27
Salisbury (Wilts), bishop of, 73, *and see* Bingham, Robert de; Bohun, Jocelin de; Bridport, Giles of; Poore, Richard; Wyle, Walter de la; York, William of
castle of, 29
cathedral of, 5, 12, 45
diocese , 5
see of, Old, 12, 29; New, 12, 29, 31
Salisbury, earl of, *see* Longespée, William
Sanchia, sister of Eleanor of Provence, queen of England, 41; wife of Richard, earl of Cornwall, 41
Sandwich (Kent), 27n.
Saxony, duke of, *see* Henry the Lion
Scotland, rulers of, 7; king of, *see* Alexander II; Alexander III; William I; queen of, *see* Joan; Margaret
Scott, Dom Geoffrey, OSB, abbot of Douai, 101n.
Seagrave, (Leics), Stephen of , justiciar, 35
'Seford' (?Sussex), 85, 89n.

Sewal, lord of Curridge, 81 and n.
Sheffield (in Burghfield, Berks), 113
Shenstone (Staffs), manor of, 112
Shottesbrooke, Elias of, 49
Showell (in Little Tew, Oxon), 123
Shrewsbury (Salop), abbey of (Benedictine), abbot of, *see* Gruffe, Walter
Sigillo, Robert de, 54n.
Simon,
  abbot of Reading, 10, 25, 31, 121
  bishop of Worcester, 54
  sub-prior of Reading, 71n.
Slindon (Sussex), 33
Siward, Richard, 35
Snowdon (Wales), 23
Soulbury (Bucks), 93n.
Southampton, Richard of, 47
Southwark (Surrey), priory of (Augustinian), annals of, 9, 19n.
Spain, 23
Stanford, Robert of, 93
Stephen,
  king of England, 1, 56, 63n.
  chaplain of Pope Gregory IX, 33
Stoke Prior (Herefs), 47, 49
Stratfield Mortimer, 123n.
Strongbow, *see* Marshal, Richard
Suffolk, 58, 75
Sulebir, Simon de, 49
Surrey, 58; sheriff of, 58, *and see* Malcuvenant, Mauger
  earl of, *see* Warenne, John de
Sussex, 58, 89n; sheriff of, 58, 63n.
Sutton, Richard of, precentor of Reading, 45
Sutton Courtenay, 91n.

Tarrant (Dorset), abbey of (Cistercian nuns), 39
Tew, Little (Oxon), *see* Showell
Thames, River, 11
Thomas,
  dean of Leominster, 41
  monk of Reading, 71
Torigny, Robert of, 5
Tusculum, Nicholas of (Nicholas de Romanis), bishop of Tusculum, papal legate, 25

Ugo, bishop of Ostia, *see* Gregory IX, pope
Ulster, lord of, *see* Lacy, Hugh de
Valence,
  Aymer de, bishop of Winchester, 43 and n, 45n.
  Guy de, 47
  William de, 45n, 47
Vastern, in Reading, Franciscan friary at, 35
Venice (Italy), doge of, 19

Waleby, Roger, 47
Wales, 23, 41, 43, 45
  prince of, *see* David; Llewelyn ap Iorwerth; Llewelyn ap Gruffudd
  rulers of, 7
Wallingford, 9; *and see* Fitz Count, Brian
  Ralph of, 49
Walter, Hubert, archbishop of Canterbury, 19
Warenne,
  John de, earl of Surrey (Earl Warenne), 47
  William, Earl Warenne, 39
Warin, granger of Reading Abbey, 123
Warkworth (Northants), 97, 99n.
Warwick, countess of, *see* Longespée, Ela
Wavendon (Bucks), 93n.
Waverley (Surrey), abbey of (Cistercian), 81n; annals of, 11n
Wells (Somerset), Hugh of, bishop of Lincoln, 35
Welsh, 'king of the', *see* Llewelyn ap Iorwerth
Wendover (Bucks), Roger of, 1
Westminster, 29, 31, 33, 39, 47, 49n
  abbey of (Benedictine), 101, 103
Whitsbury (Hants, formerly Wilts), 123n.
Wigmore (Herefs), William of, 45
William I, king of Scotland, 23, and n, 25; daughter of, *see* Margaret
William,
  bishop of St Andrews, 41
  boy of Reading, 75
  sub-prior of Reading, 71, 73

William, cont
the Templar, abbot of Reading, 85n, 112; archbishop of Bordeaux, 112
Wiltshire, 58
Winchcombe (Glos), abbey of (Benedictine), 39
Winchester (Hants),
annals of, 5
bishop of, *see* Blois, Henry of; Lucy, Godfrey de; Raleigh, William de; Roches, Peter des; Valence, Aymer de
Windsor (Berks), 23
Wintney (Hants), priory of (Cistercian nuns), 10
Wissant, 11, 25
Worcester (Worcs), 27, 49n.
bishop of, *see* Blois, William of; Cantilupe, Walter; Evesham, Silvester of; Mauger; St Wulfstan; Simon
cathedral of, 27, 103; annals of, 55
Wyche, Richard de, bishop of Chichester, St, 43, 49

Wyle, Walter de la, bishop of Salisbury, 47
Wymondham (Leics or Norfolk), John of, 45, 47

York, archbishop of, *see* Gray, Walter de
William of, bishop of Salisbury, 7, 45
Ysembela,
daughter of John the fisherman, 85
wife of Sewal, 81

Index to Subjects

Absolution, 105, 107
Adoration, of the Hand of St James, 73
ad succurrendum, habit, 61; monk, 121
Albs, 102, 109
Ale, *see* Food and drink
Almoner, of Reading Abbey, 7
Altar, 71; high, 101-2, 105, 107; of St James, 75; of St Mary Magdalen, 89
Annals, 1-51 *passim*, 55 and n, 111, 119n.
Anniversaries, 6, 101, 103, 105, 111
Anointing, of emperor, 21 and n; of king, 27
Antiphons, *see* psalms, canticles and anthems
Arm, of wax, 91; *see also* Illnesses and diseases
Arrow, 95 and n; called 'pila', 95 and n.
Arrow wound, 17 and n.
Ash Wednesday, 109n.
Attack, 19, 29, 47; at sea, 41

Barn, 31
Baronial discontent, 23, 47
Baronial visit to Reading (1263), 9-10, 47
Battle, 4 (Lewes), 9 (Lewes), 10 (Evesham), 11 (Bouvines), 25n, 35 (Kildare), 47 (Lewes)
Beans, *see* Food and drink
Beginning of the year, 14-15
Bells, ringing of, 101-2, 105, 107, 109
Benedictine college in Oxford, 14, 49
Birth, failure to give, *see* Illnesses and diseases
Births, royal, 19, 23, 39, 41
Bishop, see consecration of; election of; translation of; and under individuals in names index
Blessing, of abbot, 17
with relic, 83
Blindness, *see* Illnesses and diseases
Blood, 89; *and see* tears
Booty and spoils, 93
Bowels, 63
Bread, *see* Food and drink
Bridge, 11, 39
Burial, 17, 27, 39, 69; in Reading Abbey, 102, 123n.
Burning, of king's houses, 45

Calendar, 112n, 119n. *See also* dates, Easter tables
Candle, as offering, 57, 59, 71, 73, 83, 85, 87, 91; burning at Henry I's anniversary, 101, 105
Canonization, 29, 58, 89n.
Canticles, *see* psalms, canticles and anthems
Captivity, release from, 29
Capture, 19, 23, 29, 35, 41, 43, 47
Caritas, *see* Food and drink
Cartularies, 3, 53n, 54-5, 59
Carucage, 31
Castle, 31 (Bedford), 93 (Driencourt); storming of, 93
Celebration, 101, 107
Censing, 101-2, 105, 107
Ceremonial, at feasts, 111
Chamber, of Reading Abbey, 13, 45
Chapel, 19; (St Edmund's, Reading), 10, 51; of abbess of Barking, 65; of St Mary Magdalen,
near Bucklebury, 79n.
Chapter (monastic), 105, 109
Benedictine, at Reading (1277), 13-14, 49
Charters, 59, 79, 112
Chase, hunting, 81
Chastity, vow of, 37
Cheeks, of invalid, 71, 83
Choir, of abbey church, 102, 105
Christmas Day, 77
Christmas Eve, 75
Chronicler(s), 1, 5, 7, 55, 95n.
Church, parish, 85n.
Churches, goods of, 39

circumdederunt, invitatory,105
Cloister, 115
Cluniac observance, 2, 14, 77, 101
Coinage, new, 49
Collation (monastic), 119
Collects, *see* psalms, canticles and anthems
Comet, 11 and n, 31
Commemoration, of soul, 105, 107
Commendation, of soul, 101
Compensation, for damage, 27
Compline, 101, 105
Consecration, of bishops, etc., 19, 21, 35, 37, 39, 43, 45n; of church, 41; of pope, 41
Copes, 101-2, 105, 107, 117
Cornes, *see* Food and drink
Coronation, 8, 17 and n, 29, 45n.
Corpse, 89
Coughing, *see* Illnesses and diseases
Council, 4th Lateran, attendance at, 11
Council, legatine, 19 and n, 37; in Rome, 41
Cripple, *see* Illnesses and diseases
Cross, wooden, as memorial, 77, 79, 81
Crown-wearing, 33
Crusades, crusading, 7, 17 and n, 19 and n, 33n.
Cult, of St James's hand, 55-6
Cures, healings, 53-99 *passim*
Custody, royal, 10

Dates, interpretation of, 14-15
Day-dates, 15
Dearth, 39
Death, 59, 95, 97; jaws of, 91, 97. *see also* punishment
Deaths, 17, 59; records of, 7, 19, 23, 25, 29, 31, 33, 35, 37, 39, 41, 43 , 45, 47, 49, 51
Dedication, of abbey church, 4, 39, 55; of cathedral, 5-6, 27, 45; of priory, 39
Defiance, *diffidatio*, barons' (1215), 8-9, 25
imperial, 41
Deluge, 11, 35
Deposition, of emperor, 23n.
Detention, of king, 47
Devotion, 75, 95, 97; to relic, 53, 56
Diplomatic missions, 10, 11, 25
Dishes (special), *see* Food and drink
Dissolution of Reading Abbey, 102
Doctor (medical), 71, 89; physician, 81, 83, 91
Dole (monastic), 102, 107n.
Dream, 71, 73,81, 83, 87, 93
Dropsy, *see* Illnesses and diseases
Drowning, 41
Dumbness, *see* Illnesses and diseases

Earthquake, 43
Easter tables, 2, 4, 6
Eclipse, of moon, 11, 33, 45
Education, of Reading monks, 14
Effigy, of Henry I, 103
Ego dixi, *see* Psalms, canticles and anthems
Election, of bishop, 101
Entrails, *see* Illnesses and diseases
Epileptic, *see* Illnesses and diseases
Erasure, of annal, 4
Escape, from prison, 35
Exchange of money, 43
Excommunication, 23n, 33, 39
Exile, 21, 23
Expedition (military), 33n, 91 and n.
Expulsion, from England, 45
Exultabunt, *see* Psalms, canticles and anthems
Eyes, *see* Illnesses and diseases

Face, of invalid, 71
Failure, to fulfil vow, 91
to observe St James's feast, 57, 81, 93, 95
Fair, 54n., 123n.
Fast (abstinence), 65
Fealty, 95n; renunciation of, 35; *and see* defiance
Feast of St James, failure to observe, 57
Feasts, religious, 6; (monastic), 103, 105, 111, 113, 115, 117; principal double, 103, 115; secondary double, 115; in festal copes, 117 and n; in simple copes, 119
Fever, *see* Illnesses and diseases

Fidelium, *see* Psalms, canticles and anthems
Fifteenth (tax), 31, 39n (papal)
Fingall Cartulary, 1
Fire, 31, 69
Fish, *see* Food and drink
Flans, *see* Food and drink
Flight, from battle, 47
Flood, 35, 39
Foetus, *see* Illnesses and diseases
Food and drink
  ale, allowance of, 6; of Cholsey, 119
  beans, white, 115, 117
  bread (dole), 107
  caritas, 119 and n.
  cornes (food), 115
  dishes, special (pittances), 6, 111-12
  fish, 102, 115, 117; as dole, 107
  flans, 6, 115
  generals (food), 115n.
  lozenges (food), 6, 115
  malted loaves, 115
  meat, as dole, 107
  refection (refreshment), 102-3, 107
  rissoles, 6, 115, 117
  wastel-breads, 115, 123
  wine, 102, 107 and n, 111, 115, 119, 125; allowances of, 6; price of, 19
Foot, *see* Illnesses and diseases
Forgery, of charter, 54-6
Fortieth (tax), 33, 35
Foundation, of Reading Abbey, 54, 56
Foundation stones, of cathedral, 12
Funeral, 69; of Henry I, 56n.

Gems and precious stones, healing powers of, 59, 89
Generals, *see* Food and drink
Geographical extent of cult of St James's hand, 58
Geographical position of Reading, 8
Gift, of relic, 54-6
Gloria, *see* Psalms, canticles and anthems
Gold cup, 5
Graveyard, 79n.
Guesthouse, of nunnery, 65; of Reading Abbey, 83

Habit (monastic) *ad succurrendum*, 61
Hall (*aula*), of abbey, 102, 109
Hand, *see* Illnesses and diseases
Hand of St James, 1, 3, 4, 8, 17, 53-8, 73, 77, 83, 95n, 99n; as protection, 58, 95
Hangings, in church, 101, 105
Head (skull) of St Philip, 54
Heavenly bodies, 7, 11
Hebdomadary, 105, 107
Heraldic visitation, 102
Hermit, 10, 19, 51
Historians, 1
Homage, 9, 49 and n.
Horse, 81, 83
Hounds, 81; keeper of, 58, 81
Houses, king's, 47
Hunting, *see* chase

Illnesses and diseases
  arm, broken, 57, 91
  arm, withered, 57, 69, 71,
  birth, failure to give, 57, 89
  blindness, 57, 83
  coughing up, of bloody poison, 89
  cripple, 57, 87
  dropsy, 57, 63
  dumbness, 57, 65
  entrails, 73
  epileptic, similarity to, 81
  eyes, 73, 81, 83, 85; eyebrows, 71, 73
  fever, 57, 81, 93
  fever (hectic), 57, 67
  foetus, 89
  foot, of invalid, 85
  hand, withered, 73
  itching, 73
  knee-cap, 95
  labour, of birth, 89, 91
  leprosy, 79n.
  pain, 69, 71, 73, 83, 85, 87, 89, 95
  paralysis, of hand, 85
  plague, 57, 59, 65, 67n, 77, 79n.
  quinsy, 57, 67
  reason, loss of, 69
  ribs, of invalid, 69, 71
  shins, of invalid, 75
  sight, 81, 83

Illnesses and diseases, cont
sinews, shrinking of, 81
sleeplessness, 85
spastic, boy, 57, 75
speech, loss of, 65
spirit, evil, 95
sweating, 61, 67, 81
throat, blockage in, 67
tumour, internal, 57, 95; head, 71, 73; throat, 57, 67
vision, 58, 69, 75, 87
vomiting, 63, 89, 93, 97
withered left side of body, 85
womb, 89
see also cheeks, of invalid
Imprisonment, *see* prison
Indulgence, 79n.
Infirmary, of Reading Abbey, 13, 45; infirmarian, 7
Intercession, 101, 111
Interdict, papal, 10, 21, 25
Invasion, 23, 41
Invitatory (liturgical), 105
Itching, *see* Illnesses and diseases

Jews, hanging of, 49; killing and plundering of, 47
Justiciar, *see under names* Segrave, Stephen of

Kitchen, of Reading Abbey, 13, 45
Knee-cap, *see* Illnesses and diseases
Knighting, 31, 33, 43

Labour, of birth, *see* Illnesses and diseases
Lateran Council, 11 (1216), 25
Laudate dominum, *see* Psalms, canticles and anthems
Legates, papal, 41
Leper hospital, Reading, 79n.
Leprosy, *see* Illnesses and diseases
Lewes, Song of, 9
Liberties, of Reading Abbey, 103
Lightning flash, 5, 12, 21
Litanies, *see* psalms, canticles and anthems
Liturgy, 102
Lozenges (food), *see* Food and drink

Magna Carta (1215), 8
Magnificat, *see* Psalms, canticles and anthems
Malted loaves, *see* Food and drink
Marriage, royal, 17 and n, 29, 35, 37, 41, 43, 49 and n; others, 45, 51n.
Mass, 63, 71, 77, 85, 102, 107; Mass of the Dead, 101, 105, 109; *and see* morrow mass
Matins, 101, 105
Meat, *see* Food and drink
Medicines, 85, 89
Memorial, of miracle, 57 , 77
Midwives, 89
Miracles, 53-99, *passim*
Money-clipping, 49
Morrow mass, 102, 109 and n.

Oath, 8, 17
Obedientiaries, 7, 111
Obit, 112 and n, 119n, 121n.
Offerings, votive, 67, 93
Offertory, 102, 107
Ointments, 85
Outlawry, 31
Overflow, of river, 11
Oxen, yoke of, 79

Pain, *see* Illnesses and diseases
Paralysis, *see* Illnesses and diseases
Parliament, 45 (1258)
Patron, of Reading Abbey, 8
Pavement, of abbey church, 87, 102, 107
Payment, annual, 91
Peace, making of, 37
Peal, of bells, 107
Pension, from Leominster Priory to Reading Abbey, 13
Phantom, 69
Physician, *see* doctor
'Pila', *see* arrow
Pilgrimage, pilgrims, 58, 69, 83, 85
Pillar, 75
Pittances, *see* food and drink
Placebo, *see* Psalms, canticles and anthems
Plague, *see* Illnesses and diseases
Plasters (medical), 91
Poor, the, 102, 107, 109

Prayer, 65, 93
Pregnancy, 89
Prelates, 41
Presbytery, of abbey church, 63, 102
Presta domine quesumus, *see* Psalms, canticles and anthems
Prison, imprisonment, 21, 23, 25, 35
Procession, 65, 73, 75, 115
Propaganda (for St James's hand), 58
Psalms, canticles and anthems,
antiphons, 101, 105, 107
canticles, 101, 107
collects, 101, 105, 107, 109
Ego dixi, canticle, 107 and n.
Exultabunt, psalm, 107 and n, 109
Fidelium, collect, 105
Gloria, 105
Laudate dominum in sanctis eius, psalm, 107
litanies, 65
Magnificat, 105
Placebo, antiphon, 105, 109
Presta domine quesumus, collect, 105
psalms, 101-2, 105, 107
Redemptor, offertory verse, 102, 107
Subvenite, responsory, 107
Verba mea, introit, 105
Pulpitum, *see* screen
Punishments
death, 95
hanging, 31
starvation, 23
Purgatory, 105
Purification, personal, 91

Quinsy, *see* Illnesses and diseases

Ray, of sun or lamp, 85
Reading Abbey, church, *see* altar; choir; presbytery; screen; seats; tomb of Henry I; tower
Reading Abbey,monastic buildings, *see* chamber; cloister; guest house; hall; kitchen of; pavement of
Reason, loss of, *see* Illnesses and diseases
Rebellion, 95n.
Redemptor, *see* Psalms, canticles and anthems
Refection (refreshment), ***see*** Food and drink
Reform of the Church, 11; of laws of England, 45
Relics, 1, 8, 17, 53-4, 97; gift of, 54-6; list of, 53n; swearing on, 75n.
Reliquary, of St James's hand, 5, 57, 65, 71, 75, 77, 83
Removal, and restoration, of St James's hand from Reading Abbey, 55-6
Requiem eternam, 105
Resignation, of abbot, 4; of legate, 29
Responsory (liturgical), 105, 107, 109
Re-vesting, 107
Ribs, of invalid, *see* Illnesses and diseases
Rissoles, *see* Food and drink
Rogation Days, 109

St James, picture of, in Reading Abbey, 77; altar of, in the Abbey, 75
Salt, payment in, 58, 63
Screen (*pulpitum*), of abbey, 83
Seats, stalls, 101, 105, 107
Seduction and abduction, of a girl, 71
See, episcopal, removal of, 12, 29 and n.
Septuagesima, 109
Sext (monastic), 107
Sheep, milking of, 59, 69
Sheepfold, 69
Shins, of invalid, *see* Illnesses and diseases
Ship, loss of at sea, 11, 25
Shrines, 69, 75, 83, 87
Siege, 31, 35, 93
Sight, of St James's Hand, 73
Sight, *see* Illnesses and diseases
Signing with St James's Hand, 73
Sinews, *see* Illnesses and diseases
Sleep, 61, 63, 69, 87, 89, 91
Sleeping outdoors, 65
Sleeplessness, *see* Illnesses and diseases
Spastic (boy), *see* Illnesses and diseases

Speech, *see* Illnesses and diseases
Spirit (evil), *see* Illnesses and diseases
Spoils, *see* booty
Stag, 81
Starvation, *see* Punishments
Stepmother, 87
Subvenite, *see* Psalms, canticles and anthems
'sumer is icumen in', 9
Sweating, *see* Illnesses and diseases

Talents, parable of, 61
Taxation, papal, 39; *and see* tenth
Taxation, royal, 23, *and see* carucage; fortieth; thirteenth; thirtieth
Tears of blood, 83
Tenth (papal), 33
Thirteenth (tax), 19, 21, 37
Thirtieth (tax), 39
Throat, *see* Illnesses and diseases
Timber, shifting of, 56-7, 77-8
Tomb, of Henry I, 101-3, 105, 107; location of, 102
  of King John, 103
Tonsure, shaving of, 109, 123
Tournament, 41
Towels and linen dressings, 71
Tower, of Reading Abbey church, 12, 21
Tract (monastic), 107
Translation, of bishop, 41
  of saint, 27, 29, 43, 49
  of St James's hand to new reliquary, 83 and n.
Tumour, *see* Illnesses and diseases

Vengeance, divine, 95n; of saint, 56, 81; of the Lord, 81
Verba mea, *see* Psalms, canticles and anthems
Vespers, 101, 105
Vestments, see albs; copes; habit (monastic)
Victory (in battle), 47
Vigil, 81, 101, 103, 107, 123
Violent behaviour by invalid during cure, 87
Vision, *see* Illnesses and diseases
Vomiting, *see* Illnesses and diseases
Vow, 57, 81, 83, 85, 91, 97

War, 17, 27, 33 39
Wastel-breads, *see* Food and drink
Water of St James, 57, 61- 93 *passim*
Water of St Thomas, 57n.
Weather, reports of, 5, 7, 11
Wheat, price of, 19; crop of, 39
Whirlwind, 12, 21
Wind, 31
Wine, *see* Food and drink
Witnesses, of cure, 97
Womb, *see* Illnesses and diseases
Wounding, mortal, 41